SPARE PARTS

from peg legs
to gene splices

Wendy B. Murphy

Twenty-First Century Books   Brookfield, Connecticut

Acknowledgments

American Association of Orthodontics; Cure Paralysis Now on-line; Food
and Drug Administration, The Center for Devices and Radiological
Health on-line; International Society for Hair Restoration Surgery on-
line; Mayo Foundation for Medical Education and Research on-line;
National Library of Medicine, Grateful Med, Lonesome Doc on-line; *New
York Times* on-line; *Scientific American* on-line; Shriners Hospital on-line;
UNOS on-line

Published by Twenty-First Century Books
A Division of The Millbrook Press, Inc.
2 Old New Milford Road, Brookfield, Connecticut 06804
www.millbrookpress.com

Library of Congress Cataloging-in-Publication Data
Murphy, Wendy B.
Spare parts : from peg legs to gene splices / Wendy Murphy.
p. cm.—Includes bibliographical references and index.
Summary: Discusses historic and modern devices and other means of replacing
damaged or missing parts in humans, including organ transplants, genetic
engineering, and computer-engineered limbs.
ISBN 0-7613-1355-9 (lib. bdg.)
1. Prosthesis—Juvenile literature. 2. Artificial organs—Juvenile literature.
3. Transplantation of organs, tissues, etc.—Juvenile literature. [1. Prosthesis.
2. Artificial organs. 3. Transplantation of organs, tissues, etc.] I. Title.
RD130 .M87 2000   617.9—dc21   00-020883

Photographs courtesy of North Wind Picture Archives: pp. 10, 45; Photo
Researchers, Inc./Science Source: pp. 14 (SPL), 17 (National Library of
Medicine/Mark Marten), 18 (SPL), 39 (Sheila Terry/SPL), 42 (SPL), 74 (© Hank
Morgan), 87 (James King/SPL), 129 (© 1993 David Weintraub), 141 (James King-
Holmes/SPL); Custom Medical Stock Photo: p. 33 (© 1993 J. Fishkin); Otis Historical
Archives/National Museum of Health and Medicine: p. 36; The Image Works: pp. 61
(© David Lassman), 82 (© Michael Schwarz), 138 (© J. Griffin); Peter Arnold, Inc.: pp.
64 (© Jim Olive), 101 (© Volker Steger); Visuals Unlimited: pp. 67 (© SIU), 68 (© Dell
R. Foutz), 90 (SIU), 95 (SIU); © Yoav Levy/Phototake: pp. 71, 125

CONTENTS

INTRODUCTION

In 1997 the U.S. Food and Drug Administration (FDA) convened a conference to consider "future trends in medical device technology."[1] They gathered fifteen participants, including several of the nation's leading physicians, engineers, and futurists, to identify the trends and predict the developments that would define the coming decade in health and medicine. All of them foresaw a world in which the boundaries between biological systems—our bodies—and engineering systems—manufactured parts—would become increasingly blurred. In other words, they predicted that humankind would have available a hitherto unimagined array of artificial parts to assist medical specialists in repairing the myriad things that can go wrong in the body. Bioengineered parts will, in the not-so-distant future, replace damaged joints, weakened bones, disabled nerves, failing senses, disfigured features, faltering organs, and scrambled genes.

Since that conference took place, some of their predictions are already bearing fruits. We are thrilled to read of implantable devices to alter the tremor of Parkinson's disease and microchips to restore aspects of declining memory. We also watch in awe as geneticists involved in the Human Genome Project map the blueprints of all of the estimated 80,000 genes in the body—the essential first steps in being able to correct the faulty gene sequences responsible for more than 4,000 known human genetic diseases.

In the chapters that follow, you will learn the fascinating history of the events that have brought us from the earliest artificial limbs and organ transplants to the latest developments in plastic surgery, neural prostheses, tissue engineering, gene splicing, and the use of fetal stem cells. You will also learn some surprising, sometimes amusing, facts about the ingenious devices and treatments that have been invented to "fix" baldness, hearing loss, bad teeth, big noses, deaf ears, fat thighs, and lost voices. Some of the details are gory and painful, but they must be told as context, for bloody warfare and disease and suffering have often inspired great and important discoveries. And a few of the stories verge on the bizarre or on science fiction, because medical history and technology sometimes arise from beyond the world of conventional sciences.

Lastly, there is another, more thoughtful side to the subject of artificial body parts and transplants, and we hope you will consider that as well: With every advance science makes in preserving and improving life, we inevitably "play God," deciding what is good or necessary for society. Come with us now as we describe the unique personalities and historic developments that have brought us to this unsettling moment in time. And as we get there, we will also propose some of the interesting ethical and social dilemmas that arise when humans find themselves in the position to make such changes in the natural order of things.

1

STICKS AND STONES AND SEVERED BONES

The Greek writer Herodotus left us the earliest historical record of a body part made by a human. Writing in the fifth century B.C., Herodotus tells the astonishing story of the Persian soldier Hegistratos of Elis, who upon finding himself captured and with one foot held fast in an iron cuff, devised a desperate means to secure his freedom. "Since not only was his life in danger, but he . . . would have to suffer torments of many kinds before his death, Hegistratos obtained a knife with which he cut off the front part of his foot leaving only the heel.[1] Thus able to slip out of his chains, and bleeding profusely from his bony stump, the Persian limped some 30 miles (48 km) to Tegea, where he had a wooden foot fashioned. He then returned to the fighting.

The world of surgery and rehabilitation engineering have come a long way since the days of Hegistratos. In the centuries of medical discovery and innovation that separate our day from his, later generations of tinkerers and scientists have not only improved the techniques for removing injured, missing, and diseased parts of the human body, but they also have come up with devices of increasingly sophisticated design and functionality to make us whole again. And not just for legs and feet, arms and hands. Today, with the exception of the human brain, there is not a single body part, large or small, that cannot be replaced with artificial or borrowed human and animal parts. Eyes, teeth, hearts, and livers are now transplanted with almost routine regularity. And probably, in the near future, we will be regenerating actual human nerves and muscles—even whole body systems—that are barely distinguishable from the normal, natural organs that nature intended.

in the beginning

We know for sure that artificial legs, or prostheses in technical terminology, have been made and used for more than 2,000 years. The earliest example is a bronze, wood, and leather-strapped leg discovered in 1858 in a Roman tomb in Capua, Italy, supposedly made around 300 B.C.[2] We read that a century later, the Roman general Marcus Sergius, after being severely wounded in the Punic Wars, had his right hand amputated. Undaunted, the general reportedly had an iron hand made to replace the lost part and returned to battle, grasping his shield with the iron hand and wielding his sword with the unharmed left hand.[3] But Marcus Sergius's rigid hand was not good enough for every task, or so his countrymen thought. When the retired general wanted to become a priest, he was rejected on the grounds that a priest needed two "normal" hands to perform his duties, making him perhaps the earliest recorded victim of discrimination against the handicapped.[4] Marcus Sergius then entered government service, where he distinguished himself as an "even-handed" arbitrator of civilian disputes.

None of these Roman devices, however, mark the earliest use of replacement parts, or of bracing and supporting devices (technically termed orthoses). Cave-dwelling

Neanderthals are thought to have adapted forked branches and wooden stumps to aid the handicapped in walking.[5] And by the time of the ancient Egyptians, nearly 5,000 years ago, bamboo splints were used to brace deformed legs and wooden crutches to assist those who could not walk. Wooden legs and feet are also mentioned frequently in Nordic sagas, in the Torah of the Jews,[6] and in the Rig-Veda, the ancient and sacred poem of India.[7] On the other side of the world, the indigenous Moche people of Ancient Peru used leather-topped peg legs to support the occasional legless member of the community, as illustrated in their pottery. Clearly, the desire to be whole and the need to contribute to the life of the community are fundamental aspects of human personality and social order that go as far back as our humanity.

Surprisingly, much of the medical progress made by the Greeks and Romans was forgotten in the early centuries of the modern era.[8] During the Dark Ages, as historians call the period of social and intellectual decline that followed the fall of the Roman Empire, many manuscripts containing valuable medical information were destroyed or lost, and few people were capable of reading the sparse records that did remain. The simplest peg legs, and probably some hooklike attachments for arms, continued to be made for the disabled on a makeshift basis, but it's safe to say that the great majority of people who lost limbs to disease or injury simply died from loss of blood, infection, or an inability to provide for themselves in a world that could offer them little comfort.

There was one bright spot in this picture, and it developed in the courts of Europe's feudal princes, where the rich and powerful played at the dangerous game of jousting and swordplay on horseback.[9] Despite the sturdy suits of armor that the swashbuckling knights wore into battle, injuries, including broken bones and loss of limbs,

*Peter Stuyvesant, the last Dutch governor of New
Netherland (New York), was famous for his wooden "peg"
and his bad temper.*

were frequent. Those warriors who were lucky enough to survive amputations could afford the services of the cleverest craftsmen in the land to make them fit to fight again. And who, indeed, was better suited to the task than the armorers? Armorers had to be familiar with the movements of the human body. They also knew the characteristics of various metals and methods of joinery to make the segmented suits of armor and the finely balanced weapons for which they were so justly celebrated. Necessity is often described as the mother of invention, and armorers proved the rule in devising the earliest engineered artificial limbs and braces.

Armorer-made artificial legs were chiefly designed for show rather than walking. The idea was to disguise the fact that the knight had ever suffered a serious wound, for this handicap would make him seem a less fearsome adversary. Consequently, the typical medieval leg prosthesis worn by a legless knight was little more than a hollow attachment suspended from the working part of his suit of armor.[10] Fashioned with a permanent bend at the knee location and an artificial foot to fit in the stirrup, it allowed the knight to take his customary seat in the saddle. When the knight dismounted—or more usually was hoisted off the horse by a block and tackle—the rigidly angled leg was useless to support him. Off it came so that the knight could strap a more serviceable, if less glamorous, peg leg onto his stump to do the hard work of walking about.

Scholars believe that armorers also made artificial arms in the Middle Ages, but the earliest surviving examples date only from as late as the fourteenth and fifteenth centuries, the period in European history generally referred to as the Renaissance. One particularly fine example is a partial prosthesis known as the Alt-Ruppin hand, after the German town along the Rhine River where the device was later found submerged in river mud.[11] Amazingly, the iron hand had a movable wrist, a rigid thumb, and fingers that moved in pairs when one of the spring-loaded buttons at the base of the palm was pressed with the other hand.

Two centuries later artificial hands and arms were no longer novelties, and some of them were remarkably functional. Take, for example, the pair of iron hands an Italian surgeon claimed to have seen in use. The wearer had lost both of his natural hands but could, by means of his replacements, remove his hat, open his purse, and sign his name. Barbarossa, the red-bearded Greek-Algerian pirate who lost his left hand while fighting the Spanish in 1512, also wore an iron replacement. It was good enough to give him several more years of successful swordplay on the high seas. And the German mercenary Gotz von Berlichingen, who was equal parts Robin Hood, high-stakes gambler, and hired "hit man," wore a succession of iron hands after his own hand was severed by a cannon ball at the Battle of Landshut, Bavaria, in 1504.

Gotz's first prosthesis was made of wood and primitive in construction. Two later ones, each weighing about 3 pounds (1.4 kg), were masterworks of mechanical invention. With jointed fingers, and an elaborate system of internal springs, ratchets, and screws, the fingers could be made to bend and grasp even small objects. Their movements were controlled either with Gotz's good hand or by a cord at the shoulder. In these ways he could wield a lance or sword, hold a hand of playing cards, or guide the reins of his horse in battle, all of which he did with fabled skill until his death.[12] Though the craftsman responsible for these clever mechanical devices is not known, it is surmised that he was either a clockmaker or a locksmith, for these tradesmen were typically the most skilled metalworkers and engineers of the era.

Plastic and reconstructive surgery to repair physical injuries and deformities is also a skill with a long history. The practice was first recorded in the literature of Ancient India, where its principal use seems to have been to rebuild oddly shaped or severed ears and noses.[13] Reconstruction of ears came first. That's because early Hindus were in the habit of piercing their ear lobes and enlarging the holes to hold amulets, or charms, against evil powers. Unfortunately, this type of ear piercing often led to rips, infections, and deformities. In one of the oldest medical texts ever written, the Sushruta Samhita (about 1000 B.C.), 15 different methods for repairing a damaged ear are described.[14] Many of them are not much different from methods used by today's plastic surgeons to repair external ears.

As for noses, these facial prominences might be sliced off as punishment for a variety of sins, from excessive gossiping to the commission of adultery.[15] Whatever the causes, the punishment was common enough that more than 3,000 years ago Indian physicians developed a form of reconstructive surgery to reverse the damage, a forerunner of today's rhinoplasty. For best results, the patient had first to rescue his severed nose and deliver it to the doctor. Then, according to the written directions that survive to this day, the surgeon took "the leaf of a creeping vine, long and broad enough to fully cover the whole of the severed part" and placed it temporarily on the patient's forehead, the stem down over the bridge of the nose.[16] After tracing the leaf, the surgeon peeled back the flap of skin within the outline, leaving only the narrow "stem" of the flap still attached at the point just above the bridge of the nose to keep it alive and supplied with

13

An engraving showing Tagliacozzi's work

essential blood. Twisting the attached flap so that the top of the skin faced outward once again, he clapped the severed nose back in its original location and stretched the new skin flap taut across to adhere to either cheek. Finally, he bandaged the transplant tightly to the head, keeping only the nostrils open for breathing by means of two inserted straws. In a few weeks, if all went well, the nose graft would attach firmly and the peeled forehead would grow a new layer of skin.

Whether Western physicians had any first-hand knowledge of Indian plastic surgery is uncertain, but in the fifteenth century a dozen or more European surgeons were noted for performing nose reconstructions.[17] The need, this time, was not to replace noses taken in punishment but to reconstruct noses injured in duels or deformed by syphilis, a wide-spread and highly disfiguring disease of the era. Under the headline "How to make a new nose for someone if it has been lopped off and the dogs have eaten it," a German manual published in 1460 gives first-time surgeons several bits of practical advice: "Let nobody watch, and make the patient swear to tell nobody how you cured him. Then give him your estimate. If he wants to risk the treatment and can stand the pain, tell him how you will go about it . . . and how long he must lie still."[18] The manual also cautions surgeons not to get drunk and not to eat onions immediately before grafting a new nose, for fear such transgressions would cause him to spoil the work.

The method of nose reconstruction that seems to have been followed most widely in this era was developed by an Italian who is widely hailed as the "father of modern plastic surgery," Gasparo Tagliacozzi (1546–1599).[19] Tagliacozzi's nose repair was usually done in six sessions over a period of three to five months. Instead of the forehead flap favored by the surgeons of Ancient India,

Tagliacozzi borrowed a flap of skin from the patient's upper arm, presumably to avoid scarring the face. To preserve the flap's blood supply until the nose graft was secure, one end of the flap was left attached to the upraised arm even while the rest of the flap was stretched across the nose area. To hold this awkward arrangement securely in place, Tagliacozzi strapped his patient's head and arm together by means of a leather harness for 14 days.[20] Once the flap had taken root in its new location, it was severed from the arm. The surgeon was then able to begin reshaping it into the semblance of a nose.

As Tagliacozzi's fame spread, patients reportedly traveled from all over Europe to seek his help. But he and his fellow plastic surgeons were not without their critics, especially the fathers of the Catholic Church, who declared that improvements in the human face were blasphemies against God. Their displeasure with his nose repairs followed the talented Tagliacozzi even to his grave, when his body was denied a Christian burial. Not surprisingly, other surgeons took the Church's cue. Reconstructive surgery fell out of favor generally, not to be retrieved for several centuries.

wartime and amputations

As reported earlier, Gotz von Berlichingen lost his hand to a well-placed cannonball, a relatively new hazard in his time. But as gunpowder became more widely used, the numbers of battlefield injuries and follow-up amputations grew increasingly common. Terrible as it was, the carnage proved a boon to surgical knowledge and medical treatment, as has virtually every major war since.

The distinguished work of Ambroise Paré (1510–1590) is a particularly good example. Paré, was a barber-surgeon in the French Army.[21] This professional combination of skills required fine cutting instruments. Over his 80-year

16

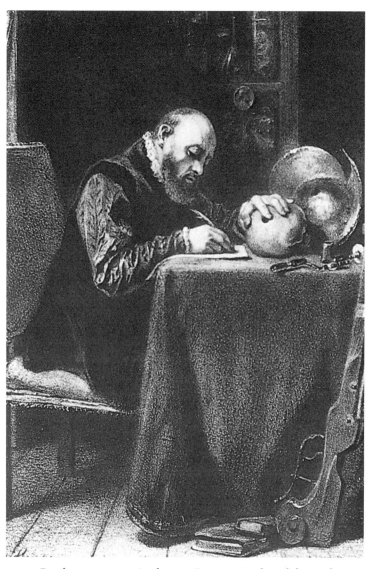

*Barber-surgeon Ambroise Paré is justly celebrated
for his skill in treating battlefield injuries and amputations. He urged his colleagues not to rely on ill-informed
classroom instructors, but to "use the eyes and hands"
to become better surgeons.*

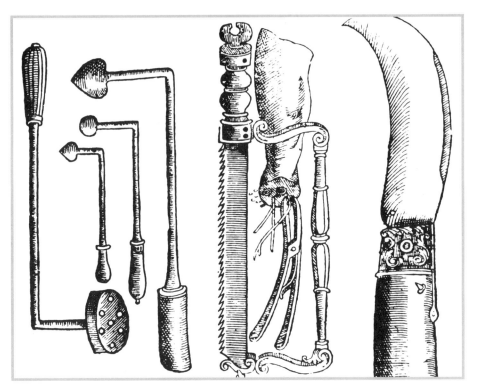

Amputation devices used in the 17th century include a knife, bone saw, clamps, and cautery irons, heated to red-hot to close large wounds.

life, Paré acquired considerable wartime experience, serving the military ambitions of five French kings through a series of bloody wars in which the good doctor had a chance to confront a wide range of surgical challenges. Because he had no formal medical training and was unable to read the traditional Latin textbooks in which most medical knowledge was recorded, Paré had to learn by trial and error. This practical experience showed him that much of what passed for medicine in his day was misguided, often making the patient worse rather than better. He especially disapproved of the way surgeons traditionally performed amputations. Paré thought that the approved methods, brutal at best, caused the patient to lose too much blood and promoted inflammation and infection.

Paré was right on all counts. One of the fundamental problems in doing any successful amputation is cutting through the many arteries and veins that run through the arm or leg. Once cut, these circulatory channels bleed until they either contract or clot at the site of injury, or the surgeon does something to close them artificially. The speed with which the blood flows out of a severed vessel depends on the type it is. The arteries tend to spurt blood, because the blood they carry is pumped under high pressure from the heart; the veins, which return blood to the heart and lungs, characteristically lose blood in a steadier, smaller stream; and the tiny capillaries that shunt blood between arteries and veins lose blood by oozing relatively slowly. The closer to the heart an amputation is made, the greater the number of vessels and the larger the diameter of the vessels that must be cut, so it stands to reason that an amputation above the knee or elbow typically poses a greater risk of rapid blood loss, or hemorrhaging, than one close to the foot or hand, and so on. Rapid blood loss can quickly lead to shock and death; it also obscures the area the surgeon is trying to repair, so that even the most skilled surgeon must always be concerned with finding ways to stop the flow as promptly as possible.

In Paré's day, the principle treatment for stopping blood loss was cautery. Cautery, which is not unlike searing rare meat on a high flame to seal in the juices, consisted of closing a wound with boiling oil, molten pitch, or a red-hot poker.[22] While this agonizing treatment often achieved its stated goal and may even have reduced the risk of infection and blood poisoning, the patient had third-degree burns to contend with on top of his original injury. Once the burns healed and the resulting scab fell off, it was not uncommon for the primary wound to start bleeding all over again. Instead, Paré recommended ligature, a method of closing blood vessels by clamping and then tying them closed, vessel by vessel, with lengths of silk thread or human hair.

It was admittedly a painstaking procedure, requiring as many as 50 separate ligatures. To aid the surgeon, Paré devised a special tool, aptly called a "crow's beak," by which to draw each vessel out from the flesh of the arm or leg stump just far enough to reach and tie it off.[23] Paré's reputation for success in controlling bleeding gradually caught the attention of his peers, and he published his detailed findings in numerous influential treatises so that other surgeons could copy him.

Paré also had nontraditional ideas about the kind of ointment that should be used to heal amputations. He recommended that the stump of an arm or leg left after amputation be treated with a gentle salve made variously of "fat of puppy-dogs," or egg, oil of roses, and turpentine.[24] Either sounds peculiar today, but they were almost certainly less destructive, and certainly less painful, than the salves his peers favored, which were loaded with arsenic, mercury, and lead. But even more important for our story, Paré devised what appears to be the first artificial leg capable of bending at the knee and ankle. Paré's leg, which was made of wood, metal, and leather, could actually be walked on with something approaching a normal gait. Though he made no attempt to make the leg look natural, he did equip it with knee lock control, a movable foot, and other engineering features that are used today. Paré also designed a flexible arm with a spring-operated elbow that bent by releasing a lever, a mechanical hand, artificial eyes, and a set of false teeth— all remarkable advances for their time.[25]

A simple fracture of an arm or leg is a relatively minor medical event these days. That's because X rays and other imaging devices reveal the nature of the problem almost instantly and lightweight casts and braces hold the bones together until they heal. Even a compound fracture, in which one or more pieces of bone break through the skin, rarely presents a medical emergency, because modern medicine has antibiotics with which to ward off the infections that once made these injuries potentially deadly. Often the break and repair are treated by a general practitioner or family doctor, though an orthopedist—a specialist in musculoskeletal disorders— may be called in. Musculoskeletal problems that cause the body's bony framework to bend unnaturally are also fairly routine today. Such congenital conditions as scoliosis (a spine that takes an unnatural curve) and club foot (a foot sufficiently deformed to inhibit normal walking) both respond well to braces and exercise when managed by doctors trained especially in these areas.

In Paré's time, by contrast, broken bones, dislocations, and skeletal deformities were treated very differently by persons known as "bonesetters."[26] The results might range from permanent disability to death. (An indication that the lame and the paralyzed were numerous is evident in the paintings of Paré's contemporaries Peter Brueghel and Hieronymus Bosch.) The bonesetter probably had no formal medical training and was either a veterinarian or even a blacksmith. The chief requirement of the bonesetter was physical strength—to pull the bones back into line—though a certain amount of intuition helped. With X rays many centuries in the future, the only way to assess the size and shape of a simple fracture was for the bonesetter to locate the break by touch, feeling it through skin that doubtless was swollen by the time the injured person was treated. And once the broken or dis-located parts were realigned, there was little treatment available—other than bandaging the area very tightly and perhaps applying a simple wooden splint—to hold the parts together while they fused. Tight bandages carried a serious risk, too, for they tended to cut off circulation. As for compound fractures, about the only treatment was amputation above the break. With antibiotics and sterile operating conditions unknown, the incidence of infection and fatal gangrene was high.

One of Paré's contemporaries, Girolamo Fabricius, thought of the next best thing. Although he could not make bones heal more perfectly, given the few tools at hand, he devised a means to brace the broken and deformed limbs so they could be at least partially useful.[27] Fabricius did not consider himself an orthope-dist, for neither the term nor the medical specialty had yet been invented, but his ideas on using form-fitting metal orthoses, or braces, were a significant step toward the creation of that specialty.

Like the early prosthetics worn by combat-tested knights, Fabricius's braces appear to have been made by armorers, but instead of the usual decorative metalwork and solid construction associated with protective body armor, his bracing "suits" were largely "see-through." Strong enough to support an arm or leg, they had plenty of open spaces between the iron straps and bars to make them lighter in weight and more comfortable for ordinary use. The sturdy braces were punctuated at strategic loca-tions with thumb screws, springs, latches, and straps, so that tension and fit could be adjusted as the body pre-sumably straightened and gained strength. There's little doubt that they were uncomfortable, but as the alterna-tives were far worse, patients apparently went along with them.

The term "orthopedics" was coined by Nicholas Andry, a French professor of medicine, in 1741, several generations after Fabricius's death.[28] Professor Andry made up the word from two Greek word roots: *orthos*, meaning straight, and *paideia*, referring to the raising of children. Andry thought, quite correctly, that the best time to correct curvature of the spine, club feet, hip dislocations, and other birth deformities was when children were very young and their growing bones and muscles more amenable to reforming. He used as his homely example an image that every gardener could relate to— that of a crooked young tree lashed to a straight staff. Braced in this way for a time, the sapling was almost certain to improve its "posture," as does the youngster with scoliosis or feet that are turned in or out awkwardly. To this day, Andry and his crooked tree remain symbols of orthopedic medicine, and his textbook, the first book devoted to the subject, is considered a medical landmark.

A British contemporary of Andry's, London surgeon William Cheselden, popularized an important advance in the splinting of deformities when he showed surgeons how to make a primitive sort of rigid cast. Writing of his discovery, he said that when he was presented with a child who had club feet, he first considered the standard bandaging technique. "Yet [this method] was not without fault, as the bandage harmed the leg and made the foot's upper part swollen." Then he remembered a novel method he had observed as a boy when a village bonesetter had fixed his broken arm, and he decided to apply it to his own patient. "The foot was restored [to a normal position] and fixed with rollers in a mixture of egg-white and wheat flour. They dried stiff and held the foot in place. I can think of no better way to fix fractures."[29]

More than a century later, a Belgian named Anthony Mathijsen did in fact find a better way: quick-drying plaster of Paris. This pastelike concoction of lime, sand, and water, invented in Paris, made it possible for orthopedists to safely encase and immobilize broken and deformed arms and legs while they healed.[30] Plaster casts have been a mainstay of orthopedic treatment ever since.

james potts's big step forward

Progress on surgical amputation and on artificial replacement parts continued slowly to the nineteenth century. As before, improvements came largely in response to the increasingly bloody warfare that kept surgeons supplied with a steady stream of patients in desperate need of help. In 1812 at the height of the Napoleonic Wars, the French Army's chief surgeon, Dr. Dominique Larrey, purportedly performed an amputation roughly every seven minutes during one particularly horrific battle on the Russian front—a total of more than 200 surgical procedures in the first 24 hours of fighting.[31] Such speed certainly did not encourage fine technique, but considering the excruciating pain experienced by patients without benefit of anesthesia, lack of technique was not their only problem. It was Dr. Larrey, incidentally, who also introduced "flying ambulances" to the battlefield.[32] In previous wars, the wounded were left where they fell until the fighting was over, but Larrey mobilized teams of stretcher-bearers to bring the wounded in for treatment immediately. Though Larrey did not know precisely why patients cared for in this manner succumbed to infection less often, his record of mortality following amputations was distinctly better than that of his predecessors.

As had been true for so many centuries before, most of the men who survived amputation in 1812 were lucky to be outfitted with even a simple peg leg, a crutch, or perhaps an immovable hook to replace a missing hand.

But three years later when Britain's Marquis of Anglesea lost a leg in the Battle of Waterloo, he wanted something better, and he had the money to pay for it. Anglesea approached James Potts, a skilled London craftsman with a reputation for making better-than-average wooden legs. The Marquis asked the limb maker to stretch his imagination and ingenuity further. In a few months Potts came back to his patron with what has since been celebrated as the "Anglesea Leg," the first truly flexible artificial leg. In addition to a hinged steel knee and ankle joint, the custom-made prosthesis had an ingenious "toe-lift" mechanism. As the knee bent to walk, artificial tendons of cat gut running down the hollow center of the lower leg contracted to lift the front of the wooden foot. Though the toe lift made a loud clapping noise with each step, it was clearly a major improvement. Not only did it reduce the risk of catching the front of the shoe and tripping the wearer when he was walking on uneven ground, but it also allowed for a more natural walking stride. The Marquis was apparently well satisfied, for he reportedly wore the new-fangled leg until he died at the age of 85.[33]

The idea behind the Anglesea Leg was soon adopted by other craftsmen, and in 1839, William Selpho, one of Potts's apprentices, brought the design to the United States, where peg legs had been the standard.[34] (Remember such great characters as Peter Minuit and Captain Ahab?) Settling in New York City, Selpho modified the English invention by inserting a rubber plate at the ankle to soften the impact of walking and by adding a rubber sole to improve traction on wet surfaces. One of Selpho's early clients was Dr. Benjamin Palmer of Philadelphia. After wearing the leg for some time, Palmer decided to try some improvements of his own, and he came up with a hardwood leg that had Potts's toe lift and Selpho's shock absorbers but with greater springiness in its step and a remarkably realistic appearance, down to

25

its shape and flesh color. Awarded the very first U.S. patent for an artificial limb, Palmer was able to license his invention to several small New England craft shops where it was manufactured for many years as the "American Leg."

Still more progress in this department was claimed by A.A. Marks, also of New York City, and Douglas Bly of Rochester, New York. Marks, who had a full line of devices for the disabled, including a "rolling chair" on wheels and a hand-propelled tricycle, also held a patent on the first prosthesis to feature a sponge rubber foot for a still softer step.[35] Unimpressed by this combination, Dr. Bly proclaimed his own prosthetic leg "the most complete and successful invention ever attained in artificial limbs." Even so, there were a few things that Dr. Bly had to admit it could not do. He declared in his catalog: "Though the perfection of my anatomical leg is truly wonderful, I do not want every awkward, big-fatted or gamble-shanked person who always strided or shuffled along in a slouching manner with both his natural legs to think that one of these must necessarily transform him or his movements . . . as if by magic, as Cinderella's frogs were turned into sprightly coachmen."[36]

Bly was acknowledging the fact that people seeking the right prosthesis to suit their special requirements continued to be on their own. Certainly the surgeons who performed the surgery had no idea. For that matter, they had little understanding of how best to amputate so that a prosthesis could later be attached with relative comfort. Unlike doctors in Europe, who increasingly were going to medical schools to get their training, the majority of American surgeons even in the larger cities had little formal medical education. Conditions were worse still in less-settled parts of the country. There, chances were good that the surgeon was entirely self-taught, that he had some other occupation, such as farming or

26

prospecting, as his primary source of income, and that he took his operating instructions directly from a book that he referred to as he worked. One surgeon's manual told the reader about to amputate a leg for the first time to gather the necessary tools and a few stout helpers to hold the patient down, and then to proceed with confidence. "Any man, unless he be an idiot or absolute fool," the author reassured, "can perform this operation."[37] One hopes the already terrified patient was spared this information at least until the surgery was over.

Amputations

Before there were artificial limbs there was amputation, the removal of a body part—typically an arm or leg—by surgery. Examples of amputations have been found in Neolithic skeletons uncovered on every continent. We also know something of how primitive surgeons carried out their operations, for some of their tools have been identified. In addition to hatchets of polished stone, some had rudimentary saws fashioned from sturdy animal jawbones, except that the teeth were replaced with sharp pieces of flint or obsidian.

Primitive amputations presented serious problems of infection, hemorrhage, and shock, due to blood loss. They were variously performed to appease the gods—what might be termed "spiritual rehabilitation"—or to punish. Lips and nose might be removed for lying, a right hand for stealing, and a foot for being lazy! And some amputations were done for the same purposes they are done today, namely to repair a wound or remove a deformed or diseased member, so that the patient could continue to function to a limited degree in the community. Gangrene, tuberculosis, and leprosy were among the ancient diseases treated by amputation. But even in those long-ago days, the loss of part of the body was understood to be an assault on the person's self-image. So, following surgery, the severed part might be preserved and set aside. When the amputee eventually died, it was restored to its rightful place in the burial pit, ready to accompany the rest of the body to the spirit world.

The excruciating pain that accompanied ancient amputations had to be tolerated in most cases. Patients who remained conscious during surgery were held down by several assistants or lashed in place with rope. Various plant-based narcotics, analgesics, and tranquilizers might be supplied if suffering and punishment were not the explicit purpose of the surgery. Early surgeons also seem to have known something about preventing hemorrhaging. They temporarily sealed bleeding arteries with a variety of primitive tourniquets, clamps, cautery (burning), and ligature (tying cut ends of blood vessels with threads made of human hair, cat gut, or natural fiber). Enough patients survived to keep surgeons trying.

The same methods of amputation continued to be followed for centuries, with small but important gains made by the Greeks and Romans. But during the Middle Ages much surgical knowledge was forgotten, new superstitions arose, and patients' chances of recovery declined sharply. One particularly astonishing development was the use of a gooey substance known as "weapon salve" to heal amputations. A concoction of ground-up mummy dust, earthworms, iron oxide, pig brain, and "moss from the skull of a man who had been hanged under the sign of Venus," weapon salve was not applied to the wound but rather to the attacker's weapon. If that could not be found, then it was smeared on the patient's bloody clothes. Even the celebrated sixteenth-century German surgeon Wilhelm Fabry of Hilden swore by weapon salve. If the goo had any medical value, it was in diverting the doctor from heaping some equally peculiar curative on the wound itself, which was better left to heal on its own.

Methods of amputation and follow-up treatment progressed in response to the changes in the nature of injuries. Gunpowder, introduced in Europe in the fourteenth century, resulted in deeper, dirtier wounds and more torn arteries and smashed bones. Amputation in these cases was almost always the only treatment offering a chance of recovery. Even then, surgeons operating before the sixteenth century rarely bothered to amputate above the knee or elbow because the numbers of arteries and the pressure of the blood was more than they could handle. Ambroise Paré was the first to figure out a way to do thigh amputations, through a method known as ligature, or tying-off blood vessels with thread, but as more than 50 ligatures had to be completed, very quickly and in the proper sequence to keep the patient from bleeding to death, few surgeons dared try it until the nineteenth century when a variety of improved surgical clamps and tourniquet aids came along. Even as late as the 1860s, the English surgeon Joseph Lister reported that 46 percent of amputees on his hospital wards died—some from infection, some from excessive blood loss, some from the sheer ineptitude of surgeons and the tools with which they had to work.

2 THE MOTHER OF INVENTION

In 1861, when the American Civil War began, the care of the sick and wounded was approaching what Surgeon General William Hammond of the Union called "the end of the medical Middle Ages."[1] In Europe the men who would someday prove that germs caused disease—principally Robert Koch and Louis Pasteur—were just beginning their investigations. And while European medical schools were justly celebrated for their scientific contributions to such studies as the circulation of the blood and the fundamentals of anatomy, most American doctors had profited little from their discoveries because information traveled very slowly across the Atlantic.

In fact, American medical schools, with a few notable exceptions, were often little better than diploma mills. Most gave out certificates of graduation in exchange for a hurried course in the most basic and often outmoded methods. American doctors, for example, still knew precious little about anatomy or the mechanics of the body—how muscles, tendons, and ligaments work with skeletal bones to provide movement. They also had scant training in pathology, the medical science that seeks the underlying causes of disease. And though anesthesia had become available to put patients out of their misery during operations, most surgeons still dosed their subjects with a shot of whiskey, a few grains of opium, or more often, nothing at all to save time. Nor did medical doctors understand the role of sterilization in preventing infection; it was rare for American surgeons to take even the basic precautions of sterilizing their bare hands, their operating tools, or the wounds they treated during a surgical examination or procedure.

The typical surgeon simply cut and slashed and sewed wearing street clothes and perhaps a bloody apron that had seen action many times without being washed. (One surgeon liked to boast that his bloody surgical garb had been handed down to him by his teacher and that, as a matter of respect, he would never wash it.)[2] The needles and thread used to sew up arteries, reattach muscles, and close flaps of skin were held until needed between the surgeon's teeth or stuck in a handy coat lapel. The bandages and plasters were often used again and again without even being laundered. This made hospitals particularly dangerous places, full of diseases that ran unchecked from patient to doctor to patient by the simple circumstance of contact. (Surgeon Oliver Wendell Holmes thought that the high incidence of deadly childbed fever in hospitals had something to do with the fact that attendants often came to a mother's bedside direct from performing autopsies and without washing their hands.[3] Fellow surgeons ridiculed the notion.)

As for preventive medicine, such as antibiotics, none were known. Most civilians made a point of having health problems attended to at home. And they avoided surgery if at all possible, regarding it as the last desperate resort of the dying.

War, however, imposes its own rules, and terrible as the bloodshed was in the American Civil War, it produced many opportunities for medical progress. By 1865 when

31

the war ended, a remarkable shift had taken place in U.S. medicine.[4] So long in Europe's shadow, American medical and surgical practices were coming of age. Soon, Americans could take pride in their countrymen's contributions. And with that shift came the beginnings of what would become American dominance in the invention and manufacture of artificial body parts, a dominance that continues into the twenty-first century.

"arms and legs in heaps"

When the Civil War began, doctors on both sides of the conflict were pressed into surgical service no matter what their knowledge or skills. They were called upon to treat huge numbers of wounded, the vast majority of whose injuries—an estimated 94 percent—were caused by gunfire of a particularly nasty sort.[5] Unlike modern steel-jacketed ammunition, which makes a relatively clean wound, the common ammunition of the Civil War foot soldier was the Minie bullet. Made of soft lead, the Minie exited rifles at relatively slow speeds. When it struck flesh, this projectile had a tendency to flatten, creating an increasingly larger hole as it penetrated and shattering any bone it chanced to meet. The resulting wounds were massive.

To make matters worse, there was no way for a doctor to find and remove the bits of broken bone, fragmented metal, and tattered uniform that were often driven inside the body along with the bullets. The likelihood of infection consequently increased with every hour that passed, so the best wisdom was to act quickly, surgically amputating all or most of the affected limb before matters worsened. Wounded soldiers were typically treated directly behind the battle lines, sometimes in tented surgical stations, occasionally out in the open; seldom were horse-drawn ambulances available to transport the men quickly to safer ground.

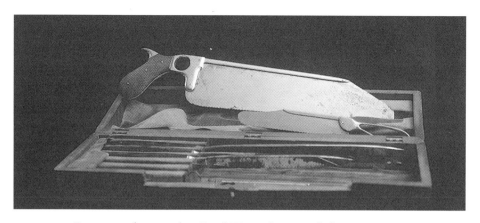

Surgeons during the Civil War often needed to amputate in the battlefield. This portable box used during the war contains bone saws, knives and scalpels.

The descriptions left by patients and surgeons of these proceedings are terrible to recount. Soldiers were readied for surgery with a dose of whiskey, opium, or, if they were lucky, a chloroform-soaked rag held to the nose.[6] But this hardly helped to dim the pain, and the harried surgeons who carried out the work were widely regarded as nothing less than torturers. A Union colonel, wounded near Baton Rouge, Louisiana, later wrote to his wife of his own experience with the dreaded "sawbones" in a candle-lit cotton mill that the medical department was using as their operating room: "On the ground lay the wounded men; some of them were shrieking, some cursing & swearing & some praying; in the middle of the room was some 10 or 12 tables just large enough to lay a man on; these were used as dissecting tables & they were covered with blood all over them & by the side of the tables was a heap of feet, legs & arms."[7]

Nearly 50 years later, another veteran surgeon of the Civil War looked back with the advantage of having learned more scientific methods in the intervening years. "We used undisinfected instruments from undisinfected plush-lined cases, and still worse used marine sponges which had been used in prior pus cases and had only been washed in tap water. If a sponge or an instrument fell on the floor it was washed and squeezed in a basin of tap water and used as if it were clean."[8] He went on to describe how in sewing up patients' stumps, the surgeons routinely used unsterilized thread, licking the ends with their own saliva to poke them through the eye of their surgical needles.

Nevertheless, the numbers of amputees who survived the war was considerable—23,000 in the Union Army alone—and this created a tremendous demand for better and more practical prostheses. Further stimulating the demand, the federal government added financial incentives to manufacturers to improve the designs of their prostheses. In 1862, Congress passed the Great Civil War Benefaction, a law that guaranteed an artificial limb for every soldier or sailor who came home so disabled.[9] In addition, an ordinary enlisted man who lost both hands was guaranteed a monthly compensation of $25 for life; loss of both feet, or one hand and one foot was set at $20. Disabled officers received somewhat more liberal pensions.

getting the hang of it

To fill the sizable need for artificial limbs, a host of new inventors got busy making improvements. Many of the tinkerers were themselves amputees who had direct knowledge of what designs worked and what didn't. One such figure was James Edward Hanger, an 18-year-old Confederate soldier who lost his leg to a Union Army six-pound shot during one of the first land battles of the war.[10] Returning to his hometown of Churchville, Virginia, Hanger made himself a leg out of a length of sturdy oak. As the leg worked remarkably well, and as he foresaw a continuous stream of amputees like himself coming back from the battlefield, young Hanger set up shop to make more.

The Virginia state legislature, impressed by the "Hanger Limb" as well as its inventor's entrepreneurial spirit, commissioned young James to manufacture legs that they would then supply to Virginia veterans. Hanger's design was based on the "American Leg," described earlier, which was considered state-of-the-art at the time.[11] Using his own experience as a guide, he devised several improvements to make the foot and ankle flex in more lifelike ways.

Another Civil War contributor was Dubois Parmlee, a New York chemist, who devised the "suction socket."[12] The socket provides the structural connection between the stump or residual limb and the prosthesis itself. Worn like a rigid sleeve over the stump, it helps to hold the prosthesis in place and is important in protecting the body from the pressure and wear that this artificial attachment can cause. Sockets are the unglamorous part of a prosthesis, much like the basement of a house is unglamorous, but they are critical to how well the whole system works.

Parmlee got his suction socket idea while thinking about the way false teeth stay in place, which is principally by suction and atmospheric pressure. He reasoned that an artificial arm or leg would hold as well as a good set of false teeth if more effort were put into fashioning the socket where the stump and the prostheses met. He turned out to be right on target, and prostheses today are fitted with this principle in mind. Parmlee also improved the shoulder harnesses, making them easier to put on and less bulky to wear. There were many other entrants in the artificial-limb competition, with some 200 clinics and 2,000 skilled mechanics working in post–Civil War America at one time.

A Civil War soldier, whose leg wound turned gangrenous before he made it to a Union hospital. Amputation was the only course to take at that point.

A few manufacturers enjoyed a lively foreign trade as well, for the new inventions quickly gained a reputation as the best in the world, and thanks to the continuing strife in Europe, demand for artificial limbs was always high. One reporter studying the situation abroad boasted that "Italian boys prayed to the Madonna for 'an American leg,'" and one French military aide on his visit to the United States, liked to claim that he was "part American" because of his wooden leg.[13]

buyer beware

Still, the situation for the disabled was far from idyllic. Surgeons continued to give little or no thought to how best to locate and shape amputations to allow stumps to bear patients' weight comfortably. Also, surgeons took no role in prescribing or fitting the prostheses once wounds had healed, so they had no chance to learn from their mistakes. Patients also received none of the aftercare—physical therapy or rehabilitation medicine—that would someday help the disabled to adapt to their new circumstances, because such services had not yet been invented. By default, limb manufacturers were left to figure out what was needed in each client's situation. While many manufacturers doubtless were well-meaning and made a serious effort to supply good prostheses at a fair price, there were also quite a few who sold poorly made products at extravagant prices. With no government watchdogs like today's Food and Drug Administration (FDA) to look after quality and shut down shoddy businesses, it was strictly a case of buyers beware.

Patients who were fortunate enough to live near a factory showroom could come in to see what was available and then be fitted if they liked what they saw. Those who lived at a distance had to weigh the evidence of the advertisements in their local newspaper as best they could, choose a manufacturer, and order the finished product by mail. Customers even had to supply the relevant measurements—size of their stump, the length of the able-bodied limb to be matched, and so on—which they or a family member were supposed to take with a tape measure or pocket ruler.

Not surprisingly, the results were often far from satisfactory. Hard to put on and take off, heavy to wear, poorly fitted, and mechanically unreliable, the replacement parts rarely lived up to their promises. Many disabled veterans learned to keep their artificial arm or leg in the closet or under the bed, to be worn only to weddings, funerals, and Sunday church services, as the saying went. The rest of the time the amputees used a crutch or a home-made arm or leg extension or even a wheelchair to get by as best they could. For all the good intentions that federal and state governments proclaimed, most disabled veterans did not prosper in peacetime. Many were forced to rely on their families or to beg for subsistence. So much that would make for happier endings a century later was still unknown and unimagined.

help is on the way

The story of the progress in repairing and rehabilitating damaged bodies must be interrupted for a moment to look once again at advances in related areas of science and technology. During the latter half of the nineteenth century, anesthesia, antisepsis, X rays, and photography all came into wide use. Each would have a major impact on the evolution of human "spare parts" as we know them.

The use of surgical anesthesia is usually dated from October 16, 1846, when William Morton, a Massachusetts dentist, was invited by the authorities at Harvard Medical

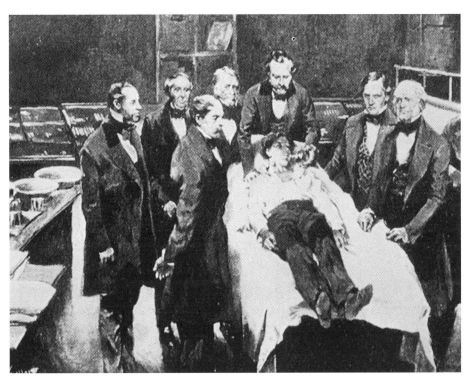

Morton's first public demonstration of surgical ether in 1846 showed that patients could be made temporarily insensitive to pain.

School to give the first formal demonstration of ether, a sleep-inducing gas, to make a patient undergoing major jaw surgery insensible to pain. (Curiously, the soporific effects of ether and nitrous oxide had been recognized for some time, and there are many recorded instances of medical students amusing themselves with "ether frolics" and "laughing gas parties," but few it seems ever considered their anesthetic potential before Morton.) A year after the Harvard demonstration, Marie-Pierre Flourens, a French physiologist, introduced yet another gas—chloroform.[14] Together, ether and chloroform provided surgeons with their first opportunity to put patients "to sleep" during operations.

Slow to be adopted, particularly in battlefield conditions, anesthesia eventually became an essential tool in surgery, one that even the most hard-hearted "sawbones" was grateful to have. With patients no longer writhing in pain, surgeons had the luxury of having time to carry out longer and more complex surgical procedures, among them amputations that were better designed to receive functional prostheses.

Antisepsis refers to scientific methods of killing infectious agents (sepsis) already present in wounds. Asepsis, its near relative, is concerned with preventing the entrance of infective bacteria into the wound during and after surgery. The problem of sepsis, which could lead to gangrene, or the death of tissue, in amputations, had bedeviled surgeons and their patients for centuries. Death rates of surgical patients due to infections ran as high as 80 percent. And the prospects for the future looked darker still, as medical care was increasingly focused in hospitals, where contamination was greatest.

Historically, physicians had used vinegar, wine, turpentine, various spices, even the resins of frankincense and myrrh, to protect wounds from infection, but with little success. Iodine, creosote, and pure alcohol were early nineteenth century additions to their surgical kits, but as surgeons continued to battle an unknown and unseen enemy, they made little progress.

One individual who gave a considerable amount of thought to dealing with infections was the Scottish surgeon Joseph Lister. The son of an amateur microscopist, Lister had an early appreciation of the work of the French experimental chemist Louis Pasteur, who had identified tiny living agents, or "microbes," as the causes of fermentation in wine, beer, and cheese. Lister eventually concluded that microbes—we now call them bacteria—were also the culprits responsible for the infections that invaded flesh wherever the normal barrier of skin was breached. He also said that many if not all of them were probably airborne.

In 1865, Lister introduced a technique he dubbed "antisepsis," by which he systematically applied a carbolic acid solution directly to the wounds and to the bandages covering them.[15] To be even more thorough, he introduced a method of sterilizing the surrounding environment by means of a mechanical atomizer. Installed next to the operating table, the hand-operated pump constantly saturated the air and everyone attending the surgery with a thick fog of vaporized carbolic acid, creating a virtual barrier between the wound and the surrounding environment. In almost no time, Lister began to see remarkable improvements in the numbers of patients who survived, and he published a series of detailed medical papers aimed at persuading medical colleagues to follow his example.

Many surgeons at first resisted Lister's recommendations. They were not convinced that airborne microorganisms were the cause of infection, and they found the new procedures awkward and unpleasant, particularly the acid-filled atmosphere of the surgical theater. But the chorus of Lister believers began to grow as the evidence mounted. By the end of the nineteenth century, antisepsis and asepsis, as well as freshly washed surgical gloves, masks, coats, and surgical tools, were widely accepted as medical necessities in most parts of the Western world.

X rays were the era's third big breakthrough in raising the success rate of human body repair. In December 1895, Wilhelm Konrad Roentgen, a professor of physics at Wurzburg University in Germany, discovered that he could photograph the bony structure of his wife's hand with the

Joseph Lister reasoned that systemic, scientifically based chemical antisepsis would improve patients' outcomes. His carbolizer, used to spray a fine mist of carbolic acid over the wound and the operative area, revolutionized surgery.

mysterious new invisible X rays. It was the first such image ever created of the interior structure of the living body. Initially, the X-ray machines were used to detect and characterize bone fractures and dislocations, but by the time the Spanish-American War erupted in 1898, they were also used to locate bullets and to guide amputation surgery.

Lastly, photography served the evolution of prosthetics indirectly by helping orthopedists to see the mechanics of human movement as never before. One of the first to undertake this study was the ever-progressive physician Oliver Wendell Holmes. Dr. Holmes noted that with his camera he was able to observe the natural motions of arms and legs in minute detail, revealing particulars never seen with the naked eye. "No artist," he wrote in wonderment in 1863, "would have dared to draw a walking figure in attitudes like these."[16]

Still more was learned through the efforts of an English-American photographer named Eadweard Muybridge. In 1877, Muybridge developed a forerunner of motion-picture photography to take fast-sequence still photographs of people and animals walking, running, and jumping. Though Muybridge's interests lay in more artistic directions, the information proved useful in developing better artificial arms and legs and better orthopedic braces, and in helping patients relearn the processes of movement. By looking at the images, they could consciously mimic ways to use their arms and legs, gestures that are easy to learn unconsciously as a toddler and young child but that can be difficult to reconstruct later in a purposeful way. In the decades to come, the study of movement and more specifically of "gait" would become an important step in fitting patients for prostheses and in restoring them to full mobility. (Gait describes how muscles, nerves, bones, and gravity work together to achieve walking movement.)

Meanwhile, warfare and its resulting injuries continued to be the major source of practical developments in prosthetics as the nineteenth century closed. One of the more important new inventions came out of the Ethiopian War for Independence. In the bloody climax of the war, fought in 1896 between the legions of King Menelik II and the Italian enemy, hundreds of Italians were taken prisoner. In retribution for years of colonial domination, the Ethiopians cut off the right hands of their captives before releasing them.

Dr. Giuliano Vanghetti, an Italian physician, wanted to do something to rehabilitate his mutilated countrymen, and he set about devising an improvement on the artificial hand.[17] Previously, most artificial hands were either movable hooks—none too pretty but functional—or they were cosmetic, approximating the appearance of a natural hand. The cosmetic hands rarely incorporated "active" features—springs and levers that readily adjusted to carry out gross movements like holding a stair banister or turning a door knob. None could do the delicate manual tasks of buttoning clothes or grasping eating utensils, activities so important to the routines of daily living.

Vanghetti conceived the idea of using the living muscles and tendons embedded in the forearm stump to operate the fingers of his artificial hand. The challenge was to find the means to connect them in such a way that they could communicate action to the artificial fingers without becoming damaged in the process. Vanghetti turned to puppetry for his solution. Known today as "kineplasty," Vanghetti's idea was to separately enclose the severed ends of each of the muscles and tendons with coverings of skin so that they could continue to execute independent movements and receive independent

Artificial Arms and Legs.

MARKS' Improved Rubber Hands and Feet are Natural in Action, Noiseless in Motion, and the Most Durable in Construction. It is not unusual to see a farmer working in the fields with an artificial leg, or an engineer, conductor, brakeman, carpenter, mason, miner, in fact, men of every vocation, wearing one or two artificial legs. of MARKS Patents, performing as much as men in possession of all their

natural members, and experiencing little or no inconvenience. Over 25,000 in use, scattered in all parts of the world. At the Paris Exposition they received the highest award. They are endorsed and purchased by the United States and foreign Governments. A Treatise containing 500 pages, with 800 illustrations, sent FREE, also a formula for taking Measurements by which limbs can be made and sent to all parts of the world with fit guaranteed. Established 49 years

A. A. MARKS, 701 Broadway, New York City

By the end of the 19th century,
many companies were manufacturing prostheses,
and advertising their wares.

sensations as they had before injury. He then planned to connect them like puppet strings to cords running to the artificial hand and fingertips.

Lacking the necessary engineering know-how to carry out the details, as well as an understanding of how to make living tissue compatible with strings or cords, the good doctor never fully succeeded in his admirable venture. However, the kineplasty concept was a valid one, and it opened up a whole new area of prosthetic research that has borne astonishing results.

out from the shadows

The years between 1900 and 1920 marked a turning point in the history of treating the disabled. New materials, new medicines, new social attitudes, and a world war all contributed to bring the West's growing population of maimed and deformed out from the shadows and into public view. Clearly, much more had to be done to make the lives of the disabled productive and satisfying.

First, there was the matter of materials. Wood, leather, and iron, the traditional materials for fabricating artificial limbs and their harnesses, had always been a problem for amputees. Cumbersome in shape as well as heavy, they added a lot of "dead weight" to the already compromised movement of the amputees who wore them. Some legs, for example, weighed as much as 20 pounds (9 kg). In 1912 an English aviator, Marcel Desoutter, who had lost his leg in an airplane accident, worked with his brother Charles, an aeronautical engineer, to come up with something lighter.[18]

Borrowing from the construction methods of lightweight airplanes, the brothers wrapped thin metal sheets of lightweight aluminum over a structural aluminum frame to put Marcel back on his feet. Encouraged by this success, the Desoutters and others also began tinkering with the over-the-shoulder harnesses by which artificial legs

46

were customarily held in place. It wasn't long before they devised waist-level harnesses that were more comfortable, cooler in hot weather, and less conspicuous. And in 1912, D.W. Dorrance, an American who had lost his right hand in a civilian accident, patented a "split hook" prosthesis.[19] While not so visionary as Vanghetti's device or as simple as the old-time hooks, it was remarkably adept at performing ordinary tasks. Dorrance's clever two-pronged appliance opened and closed to grip small objects, much as a normal finger and opposable thumb spread and come together to hold a pencil or a fork. Hinged at the base, the contrivance had a side lever that opened the pincers when pressed against a table or the body; it snapped closed with rubber bands when the lever was released.

The Dorrance hand laid the way for a generation of split hooks that would follow. In the medical sphere, the idea of rehabilitation medicine as a specialty began to take shape at the beginning of the twentieth century. Ordinary as the notion of rehabilitation sounds today, it was a radical new concept back then. Rehabilitation medicine is based upon the belief that the disabled can be made better, often even returned to normal life. But to achieve that goal it takes more than a crutch, an orthopedic brace, or an artificial leg. Rather, it takes psychological, occupational, and economic support of the patient, delivered by a team of specialists—surgeon, orthopedist, appliance manufacturer, physical trainer, social worker, and occupational therapist—sometimes over many months and even years. And it costs a lot of money, usually supplied by government or private insurance. The idea that people with disabilities and deformities could and should be rehabilitated arose for a number of reasons, but probably no factor was more important than the alarming rise of workplace accidents that accompanied the Industrial Revolution.

Crippling injuries had always plagued humans, but except in times of war, most injuries in the past had happened one by one, in scattered communities. While they were tragic for the individuals affected, they were not particularly visible to the general population. Also, there was a widely held attitude that when bad things happened to people, it was God's will, and that nothing could or should be done to change the outcome.

In the modern era, however, accidents on the job had become tragically common. High-speed, mechanized assembly lines, exhausting working hours, fast-moving transportation systems, and free-for-all business competition at any cost had created an environment in which countless accidents and mutilations were an ordinary part of workers' lives. In 1913 when the first yearly statistics on industrial accidents were gathered in the United States,[20] there were more than 25,000 fatalities and 700,000 significant job-related injuries among American workers.[21] Progressive-minded leaders everywhere began calling for efforts to impose safety rules on employers and force them and government to cooperate in keeping a census of accidents and in aiding these unfortunates. Germany led the way in enacting compulsory workmen's compensation laws, and beginning in 1908 the United States followed suit, state by state.

With funds becoming available to treat the disabled, the medical community began to take a broader role in developing wider-ranging care, including rehabilitation services. Then, along came World War I, and interest in care of the disabled truly soared. Although the percentage of battlefield amputees in this newest war was lower than in nineteenth century wars, owing to improvements in the ability to close wounds and reduce infection, the actual number of individuals who lost one or more limbs was huge because overall casualties on both sides were so high. When the fighting ended, nearly

48

150,000 civilians and fighting men had lost limbs to military campaigns.

Luckily for them, the doctors chiefly responsible for doing wartime amputations were more likely than earlier generations of surgeons to have advanced training in bones and joints and the mechanics of muscle action. This new crop of men recognized, as their predecessors had not, that they needed to be involved with the outcomes of their surgery. That meant that they were prepared to work closely with the craftsmen who made the artificial limbs and with the other rehabilitation specialists.

In the United States, the job of caring for wartime amputees was initially managed by the U.S. Public Health Service. After the war the job passed to the newly created Veterans Bureau, which ran a large number of veterans hospitals around the country. The hospitals were staffed by hundreds of young women known as "Reconstruction Aides," the forerunners of today's physical and occupational therapists.[22] Along with teaching the disabled how to move and maintain balance, the Reconstruction Aides gave their patients short courses in how to care for their stumps and for their prostheses. Soldiers who lost sight or hearing were taught how to make their remaining senses do the work of the missing eyes and ears—in effect, how to see with their sense of touch and hear with their eyes. (Guide dogs as "seeing-eye" companions for the blind were another rehabilitative aide that originated during World War I.)

Reconstruction Aides and orthopedists also progressed in the new science of "gait analysis." They studied in detail how the normal hip, thigh, knee, lower leg, ankle, foot, and individual toes connect as a unified system to take a step. Similarly, they observed the normal sequences of hand, arm, and shoulder movements involved in performing tasks like eating, dressing, and folding a newspaper. And they measured the strength and rapidity with which various muscles contracted and extended in order that the artificial replacements might better imitate them.

The artificial limbs produced during and after World War I depended on local custom and manufacturing capabilities. Among European farmers, for example, there was a marked preference for sturdier prostheses with fewer moving parts that could be worn in field and barnyard. Salesmen and office workers, by contrast, generally preferred the more finicky but less noticeable "Sunday" or "parade" limb for everyday wear. In Germany, where artificial hands of clockwork complexity had a tradition going back to the days of jousting, an engineer in Dusseldorf came up with a lower-arm prosthesis that offered clients 20 different tool attachments, "one for each of the ordinary operations of life."[23] The various parts were plugged into a universal wrist receptacle, in much the same way that a modern socket wrench or power drill has many different attachments.

Amputees were also put through programs in physical exercise and endurance training, often involving weights and pulleys, and devices were invented to measure their strength and range of motion as they progressed. This equipment would become the forerunners of the remarkable machines used today in virtually every high-school physical education department, fitness center, and rehabilitation facility.

World War I brought a sizable number of facial injuries. As skilled plastic surgery was still rare, the job of providing repairs and replacements for facial externals often required the combined services of a regular surgeon to close the wounds and a sculptor to make the attachable parts. Dr. Chavanne of Lyons, France, for example, was celebrated for the do-it-yourself ear prosthesis system he devised. Chavanne's patients were sent home with a plaster mold of the missing ear, a jar of custom-tinted plaster, and instructions on how to make fresh casts, which were generally required once a week.[24] How successful the home-made prostheses were is not recorded.

Clearly, efforts to put the handicapped back on their feet, literally and psychologically, had taken a number of new turns, but the most important one was in the attitudes and expectations of society. For the first time, the handicapped were being welcomed back as valuable members of the community, and efforts were under way to make them functional, contributing participants.

Nevertheless, that still left countless others who, because of some shortcoming of the heart or kidneys or some other organ, were being left behind. The next critical challenge lay in devising ways to repair the body's internal systems. It wasn't long before there was astonishing news on that front too.

Teeth, False and Faithful

Of all dental procedures, tooth extraction has the longest history. From earliest civilizations, the traditional way to deal with a painful, diseased, or broken tooth was simply to have it yanked out in the hope that the space would eventually heal and close over, leaving a small gap. Tooth-pullers, who earned their titles largely on the basis of physical strength, might pull a painful tooth with their bare hands, or with one of a number of handmade pliers-like tools or strings that added a degree of leverage to the task. (In many poorer countries, village tooth-pullers continue to ply their trade in this manner.) As the loss of several teeth in a row could inhibit chewing, which was and is critical to good nutrition and consequently to survival, the idea of fashioning crowns (to cover missing tops of teeth) and bridges (used to anchor artificial ivory and bone teeth in the space between two natural teeth) was devised by the Ancient Etruscans at least 2,500 years ago. Those examples that survive are made of gold, so it's likely that the rich and powerful were the primary customers of this technology.

Somewhat more successful were various attempts at filling cavities. When a tooth develops a cavity, the decayed tissue must be removed before repair is begun. Poking tools were the first devices used, and in time it occurred to someone to twirl them to effect a slow form of drilling. The first rotary dental drill, dated to 1790, is credited to George Washington's dentist, John Greenwood. The "dental foot engine" was inspired by his mother's foot-treadle spinning wheel. As for tooth fillings, everything from stone chips to turpentine resin, natural gum, gutta percha, and various soft metals including gold, silver, and lead were literally pressed into service over the centuries.

One inventive soul, the renowned sixteenth-century physician Ambroise Paré even tried plugging the holes in rotted teeth with bits of cork. But it was not until motorized dental drills were invented in the latter half of the nineteenth century that dentists routinely offered to fill diseased teeth. The first generation of these new fillings were various "amalgams" of coin silver and mercury, held in place by dental cement. Larger cavities were repaired by taking a wax impression of the hole to be filled and then using the wax model to prepare a porcelain casting, a procedure that is still followed.

False teeth, used to replace broken or diseased teeth altogether, also go back to the Ancient Etruscans, who used ivory or bone to fashion partial dentures. But as in the case of crowns and bridges, the art and craft of making false teeth largely disappeared when the Etruscan civilization declined. For many centuries thereafter, even wealthy and powerful people were accustomed to being gap-toothed. (Queen Elizabeth I is said to have stuffed the spaces between her missing teeth with bits of white cotton when she wanted to look her best.) The handful of craftsmen who did experiment with making replacement teeth generally hand-carved them from bone—elephant or hippopotamus bone were favored—or used human teeth extracted from the dead or sold off by the poor to raise cash. Ivory, another option, resisted cleaning and frequently gave off an offensive odor, which made the wearer unpopular.

Whatever the materials, early dentures had to be tied by silk thread to the remaining teeth in the customer's mouth, a rather unreliable arrangement. Sometimes, however, teeth were lacking altogether, so the denture-maker crafted a full set of uppers and lowers held together at the back by a spring-loaded hinge. The wearer had to remove them when eating. Worse yet, the dentures might jump out unexpectedly when a person laughed or coughed, a thoroughly embarrassing event. George Washington knew the tortures of false teeth; he wore a full set from middle age on, and his diaries tell us that he was rarely without discomfort. At least one set was wooden.

Modern porcelain teeth were first devised in France in the eighteenth century. By the second quarter of the nineteenth century they were available commercially at prices that made them widely affordable. At the same time, Charles Goodyear discovered vulcanized rubber, making it possible to prepare a comfortably fitting base for false teeth, and Horace Wells came up with nitrous oxide, or "laughing gas," making painless tooth extraction a reality. With this, false teeth became a common form of prosthetic improvement among those who could afford them. Less fortunate folks continued to have them pulled, pain or no pain.

A still more advanced version of dentures came along in the 1960s when a Swedish procedure known as osseointegration was developed. The jaw is drilled at each site where a tooth once grew, and a hollow threaded post of titanium or some other biocompatible material is implanted. After several months the posts are surrounded with a paste-like bony material and together they become the equivalent of tooth "roots." At this point artificial teeth capable of functioning almost exactly like natural ones can be screwed onto each post.

Orthodontics, the dental specialty involved in straightening teeth, emerged in the 1840s but was not widely practiced until after World War II. As orthodontia aims to retrain or correct existing teeth that are misaligned, it is closer to orthotics than prosthetics in its basic approach.

At the end of the twentieth century, more than 2 million Americans begin orthodontic treatment yearly to have one or more teeth "braced." Thanks to lighter materials and removable devices such as metal or plastic retainers, the process is much more comfortable and often of shorter duration than it once was.

3 PUMPS, PACEMAKERS, AND THE JARVIK-7

Looking back on what was known medically before the twentieth century, it now seems truly astonishing that physicians could do as much for the injured and crippled as they did. A skilled surgeon could usually close a severed vein with fine stitches in time to prevent too much blood loss, but fast-flowing major arteries frequently defied even the best practitioners.

The blood transfusions needed to replace substantial amounts of lost blood were rare and almost always deadly, because no one understood the role of blood "types" and blood compatibility. Without that knowledge, doctors had no clue to the basis for tissue rejection—why, for example, the skin of one person cannot be used to close the wound of another.

Another enormous problem at the turn of the century continued to be infection. Though the source of infections was beginning to be understood, control was uncertain. Without modern antibiotics, the nineteenth-century surgeon sensibly regarded surgery to repair any sort of deep-seated damage to the body as extremely risky. The very idea of touching something as delicate as the heart or liver, let alone cutting into it or replacing it with another, was beyond the imagination of most.

But in the twentieth century, new skills and knowledge developed rapidly to change the rules of the game. Along with amputation and the substitution of artificial prostheses, it has become possible to implant replacement joints, arteries, bones, and even whole organs—artificial and natural—when the body's own natural equipment fails.

The first artificial joint was tried in 1905 when J. B. Murphy, a Wisconsin surgeon, developed a replacement hip joint for a patient who had become immobilized by painful arthritis.[1] About the same time, a German surgeon attempted to replace a patient's cancerous knee joint with one taken from a cadaver. Like most new inventions, these daring procedures proved less than satisfactory to the patient, but they worked well enough to show physicians that the basic idea was sound. With further experiments, joint implants could be made to work.

The problem with joint implants is that they must not only be fixed to living bone, but in the case of hip and knee, they must flex in several directions and carry substantial loads. When an individual takes a normal step, lifting one foot while setting the other down, virtually the entire weight of the body is concentrated for a moment on the supporting leg, including the joints at the hip, knee, and ankle. (Forces nearly six times a person's body weight have been recorded during running, considerably more than that of a weight-lifter going through a lift-and-press routine!) The joints must take the weight while rotating front-to-back and side-to-side, and do it over and over, countless times, year after year, without themselves wearing down or becoming deformed. Even ordinary iron and steel machine parts can't withstand that kind of mechanical abuse for many years. From a physics point of view, how the many components of a healthy human joint do as well as they do is all quite amazing.

In the years since Dr. Murphy's first attempt at joint replacement, physicians and bioengineers have worked to solve a host of associated problems. It took many decades before they came close to a solution. The first major breakthrough was not until the 1960s. As before, it involved an artificial hip joint. The hip joint is one of the more troublesome moving body parts. Osteoarthritis, a degenerative disease associated with aging and some stressful sports, can cause the cartilage cushion between the cup-shaped socket of the pelvis (acetabulum) and the ball-shaped top of the thigh bone (femur) to become rough and pitted. Eventually, the cartilage—which itself is without the sensation of pain or pressure—wears away altogether, leaving only bits of debris in the space between the two sensitive bony components. When this happens, not even synovial fluid—the natural self-lubricating fluid that fills the remaining space—can relieve the friction and abrasion. The joint that once moved without resistance becomes stiff and barely able to rotate. As the bones grind against each other, the simplest movement becomes excruciatingly painful.

John Charnley, a British orthopedist, found a solution. Charnley had been working on the problem of what to do for patients with degenerated hip bone. His predecessors had tried a number of approaches, most involving the fixing of a ball-tipped metal shaft to the worn top of the femur by means of a stainless-steel screw. But patients still complained—their new joints squeaked with every step, the bony parts continued to deteriorate due to irritation by the foreign materials, and the screws tended to loosen with time. Sometimes, the entire hip would come apart without warning. Working like an industrial engineer to find a better way, Charnley ran exhaustive wear tests on various materials.

Eventually he settled on stainless steel for the rotating ball at the top of the thigh bone. Stainless steel has the ability to carry heavy loads and withstand wear; at the same time, because it is "stainless," it does not react to adjacent tissues and fluids. Dr. Charnley eventually chose high-density, low-friction plastic to form the corresponding cup-shaped hollow of the pelvis, where the ball joint normally rotates. Then, how to attach the cup to the supporting bone was a problem. Charnley got his answer from a professor of dentistry, who recommended a compatible adhesive that dentists use to cement fillings in tooth cavities. Charnley tested his new hip-joint implant in 1972, and when it proved to be a significant advance in design, the procedure and the device were quickly adopted by orthopedists everywhere. Success with the hip implant led to the use of artificial joints for other high-stress parts of the body.

Within two decades of Charnley's hip, the National Center for Health Statistics could report that U.S. surgeons were annually performing a half-million hip, knee, and shoulder replacements. Improvements have been made in the materials used. Implant stems—the long, slender parts inserted into long bones—are now coated with substances that are chemically so similar to natural bone that bone tissue will actually grow into the artificial stems over time, the two becoming virtually one. Consequently, it is often possible to forego the "glue" entirely.

organ music

Joints are not the only body parts to become damaged or worn out and need replacement. Whole organs can fail. When that happens, doctors have no choice but to seek a viable substitute if the patient is to have a chance at normal life. As organs, by definition, are highly complex organizations of several different kinds of tissues, all working together, medical innovators recognized that devising wholly artificial substitutes would be a difficult task. Many thought it was impossible. The best hope has always been to replace defective organs with existing healthy ones, taken from donors, live or dead.

Unfortunately, the body is not built like an automobile or other machine with easily interchangeable parts. Though components like hearts and kidneys and livers perform identical tasks from one body to the next, they each have unique genetically determined characteristics. When a donor organ is inserted into someone's body, the information that it is "foreign" is detected very quickly by the white blood cells of the body's immune system; these white blood cells react by going into attack mode, as though confronted with a deadly infection. Though experiments to resolve rejection problems had been under way with animals for several decades, the first human organs to be transplanted successfully were kidneys, the bean-shaped organs responsible for filtering and purifying the blood.

That it should be a kidney, rather than a liver or a heart, was almost a foregone conclusion. First, kidney (or renal) disease is a serious and relatively widespread health problem; it's associated with severe infections, a number of congenital and genetic disorders, diabetes, accidental poisoning, and allergic reactions to certain drugs. Second, kidney failure is usually a slow, drawn-out process, which allows doctors the time to figure out what can be done to assist the patient. Third, healthy replacement kidneys are in greater supply than other organs. This is because everyone is born with two kidneys, which is one more than they usually need. Unless something happens to injure one of the kidneys, the second kidney remains a functioning "spare." Consequently, it is often possible to get a donor organ from a willing relative. (People of the same family tend to have more genetically similar characteristics than total strangers. Brothers and sisters, for example, have a 25 percent chance of being compatible, while the chances of a good match between unrelated individuals are only about one in 1,000.)[2] And last, the surgical procedures

59

needed to disconnect and reconnect a kidney are relatively simple as organ systems go.

The landmark surgery that inaugurated kidney and all other types of organ transplants was carried out in 1954 at Boston's Peter Bent Brigham Hospital. It involved twins—one near death with two diseased kidneys, the other in excellent health with two healthy kidneys. As the twins were genetically identical—the only circumstance in which this happens—their tissues matched perfectly, and the transplant was a total success.[3] Both recipient and donor went on to live healthy lives. However, subsequent transplants between imperfectly matched donors and recipients enabled doctors to observe at close range what actually happens, and they realized more fully that incompatibility was going to be a major problem. The "stranger organs" would, in a matter of weeks or months, be detected by their new bodies' immune systems, and the tissue-rejection process would begin. The site at which the organ was attached would become intensely inflamed, and the organ would begin to separate and die.

What was needed, surgeons realized, was some kind of drug to suppress the "graft-host" activity of the immune system, without interfering with the body's other good and necessary defenses against infection. Certain corticosteroids and anticancer drugs were tried and found to be partially effective in suppressing rejection. But they risked damaging other bodily functions. Then in 1980, a drug called cyclosporine was tried experimentally. Based on a soil fungus (as is the antibiotic penicillin), cyclosporine proved to be a dramatic advance in selective immunosuppression.

From that time forward, organ transplantation began to be a practical option for tens of thousands of patients in need of help. For example, more than 11,000 kidney transplants are now performed annually in the United

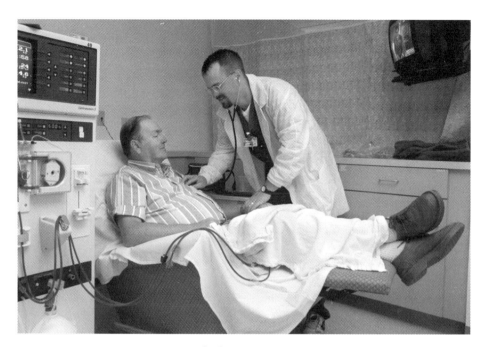

A patient receiving a dialysis treatment, where the blood is cleansed of waste products by an artifical kidney machine.

States alone, and that total would be much higher if not for the shortage of available donor organs (see Chapter 6).

Around the time that the first successful kidney transplant was recorded, kidney patients got another boost when the first "artificial kidney" was developed. A table-size appliance, the artificial kidney was capable of performing many of the same blood-purifying tasks as a natural kidney, only it did its job from a position outside the body.

The Dutch doctor Willem Kolff is credited with the basic technology (1943), but it took another twenty years to produce the workable device known as the "dialysis machine." Dialysis is basically a method of filtering the

61

blood. In one version, known as hemodialysis, two needles are inserted into permanently implanted ports or plugs in the patient's arm or leg—one in an artery to carry blood outward, the other in a vein to complete the return flow. During dialysis, the needles are connected by lengths of plastic tubing to the dialysis machine. Blood flows from the patient's artery into the machine, where it mixes with a blood-thinning drug called heparin that prevents clotting and blocking its movement. The blood mixture then travels through a coiled and perforated tube, as the small molecules of waste matter filter out through the tiny perforations while the larger blood molecules flow by. At the other end of the circuit, the cleansed blood is mixed with a second drug that cancels the blood-thinning effect of heparin and is pumped back into the patient via the vein needle. All the while, computerized controls in the machine keep blood pressure and blood temperature at normal levels.

Patients who are dependent on kidney dialysis typically undergo the procedure three times a week, for eight hours each time. In between times, they wear a short length of plastic tubing connecting the two ports on their arm so that the blood keeps flowing smoothly without interruption. As time passes, dialysis machines are becoming progressively smaller and more portable. Many patients are able to undergo dialysis at home; others go to outpatient clinics to receive the service. Today, more than 200,000 Americans depend on one form of dialysis or another for survival, with some 40,000 of them on the waiting list for a kidney transplant that could someday free them from this difficult and time-consuming routine.

the heart of the matter

Once kidney transplants had proved to be a workable idea, the way was open for other organs to be tried. The first lung transplant and the first human liver transplant were carried out in 1963. But there was one huge obstacle in the way: Much of organ-transplant surgery involves cutting and reconnecting major arteries and veins that tie the organs to the body's circulatory system. Cutting brings bleeding, often massive bleeding, that floods the site where the surgeon is trying to work. As delicate internal surgery cannot be hurried or done "in the dark," a way had to be found to slow, or better yet stop, blood flow to the area during operations. (It takes a skilled surgeon five to seven minutes to close up a congenital hole in the heart, and as much as several hours to do more complex surgery on the heart.) At the same time, blood flow must continue uninterrupted through the rest of the body—most particularly the brain—for the patient to remain alive and active.

The road to solving these conflicting requirements began many decades ago with experiments carried out by an unlikely pair of men. One was Alexis Carrel, a French surgeon at New York's Rockefeller Institute. One of the early giants of modern experimental surgery, Carrel was awarded a Nobel Prize for Medicine in 1912 for his work in animal heart transplant and for his breakthrough discoveries in methods to patch diseased human arteries with pieces of other arteries or veins. The second was Charles Lindbergh, an American mechanical engineer and aviator who is better remembered for making the first solo flight across the Atlantic in 1927.

Dr. Carrel wanted an external pump that would take over the heart's normal pumping function just during surgery. He described his idea to Lindbergh, who was never one to shy away from the seemingly impossible.[4] Lindbergh began studying the mechanics of the heart and lungs—tinkering with various ideas in 1931. Over the next four years, the engineer and the surgeon developed what they termed a "perfusion pump." This device, not unlike the dialysis machine in concept, consisted of an

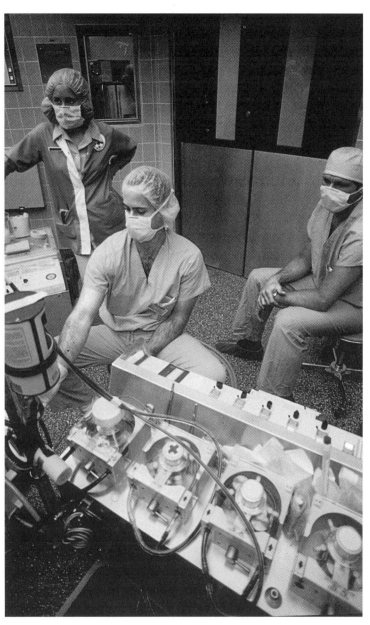

A modern heart-lung machine. Many of the mechanisms involving oxygen and blood composition are monitored and controlled by computers.

assembly of glass tubes, valves, and chambers by which blood could be diverted from the heart, circulated in a sterile, pulsating environment on a nearby table, and shunted back into the rest of the body, all the while at normal blood pressure. The glass heart proved so effective in animal experiments that Carrel foresaw a time when entire "diseased organs [or limbs] could be removed . . . and placed in the Lindbergh pump."[5] Once outside the body in a nearly bloodless environment, Carrel predicted, doctors could treat the organs aggressively, "replanting" them in the body only after they were repaired.

Carrel and Lindbergh never lived to see that day come, but others kept trying. One of these investigators was John Gibbon, a Philadelphia surgeon, who worked intensively on the problem from 1935 to 1953, and ultimately devised the first practical artificial heart-lung machine. Gibbon's device, the size of a small refrigerator on wheels, opened up a whole new field of surgical operations in which surgeons could open the heart and repair it over an extended period. With the Gibbon machine, the patient's blood was led away from the heart through thin plastic tubes to the artificial "lung." There it was suffused with oxygen molecules and relieved of carbon dioxide molecules, much as it would be in normal breathing. The blood was then drawn along through additional lengths of tubing to the artificial "heart pump," the pressure adjusted to approach normal levels, and cycled around the body.

Meanwhile, the heart itself was shocked into stillness so that repair could be carried out in relative calm. When completed, the heart was restarted with an electric shock, and normal blood flow allowed to resume. Still later, an additional treatment, known as "induced hypothermia," was added. This involved chilling the blood and body from a normal temperature of 98.6°F (37°C) down to as

65

low as 82°F (28°C), a procedure that slowed metabolism (the body's chemical processes) so that tissues and organs could survive even longer in its abnormal state. As the methods to support the heart and lungs were perfected over time, open-heart surgery became a fairly routine event.

of valves and pacemakers

No sooner had the heart-lung machine made its debut than surgeons began to tinker with faulty heart valves, the structures that stand as "one-way doors" between the heart's four chambers. When valves work properly, they open to allow blood to flow out of each chamber in response to the heart's beating or pumping and instantly close tight to prevent backwash. (With a stethoscope placed over your heart, a doctor can hear how well the valves are doing their jobs. Heart "murmurs" are sounds made by defective valves.)

Like parts in a machine pump, any one of the heart's four valves can get stuck or leak, either as the result of an inborn defect, an injury, or a disease such as rheumatic fever, which can leave a lot of scar tissue around the valves. Whatever the circumstance, the damaged heart has to work harder, and heart rhythm is disrupted. In time the heart may fail altogether. Sometimes, drugs can be used to improve the function of a faulty valve, but nowadays a replacement valve is the preferred long-term solution.

The first artificial valve, designed and implanted in 1951 by Dr. Charles Hufnagel of Georgetown University Medical Center in Washington, D.C., consisted of a 1.5-inch (3.8-cm)-long Plexiglas tube with a ball-and-cage end inserted at the valve site. As the heart pumped, the ball alternately floated free in the cage and was pressed tightly against the opening to seal it. According to Dr. Hufnagel, the valve worked no matter in what position

66

*A heart valve from a pig, which is of similar size
and structure to a human heart valve*

patients put themselves, "even standing on their heads,"
if they chose to.[6]

Mechanical valves like Dr. Hufnagel's continue to be
used today, but "biological" and "homograft" valves are
other alternatives that also have their place. Biological
valves may be harvested from pigs, whose heart is similar
in structure and size to that of humans, or from other
tissue in the patient's own body, which can be remodeled
to work like a natural valve. Homografts are removed from
the bodies of human donors who have just died. If valve
function could be improved by artificial means, medical

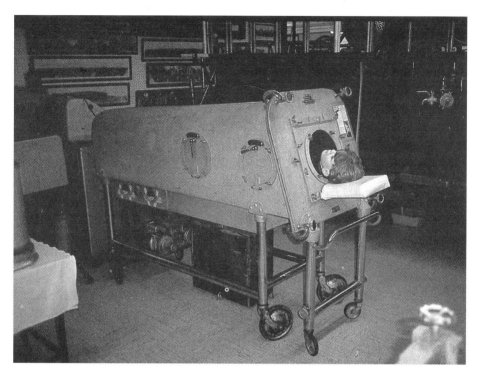

A pressurized respiration chamber, or "iron lung," for polio victims who lost the ability to breathe on their own.

researchers thought, why not other aspects of organ function, like the rhythm of the lungs and heart? Weren't these also mechanical problems, controllable by mechanical means?

One area in urgent need for mechanical assistance was the care of polio patients. Poliomyelitis was a frightening viral disease that appeared in epidemic form somewhat mysteriously in the early decades of the twentieth century and reappeared every few years with increasing severity. It affected city children in particular, though people of all ages were susceptible to a lesser degree. Polio, which was also known as infantile paralysis, often settled in the spinal cord to paralyze the muscles of breathing, leaving victims gasping for breath. Physicians tried to force air into the suffocating victims with devices similar to bicycle pumps, but they were not powerful enough.

Then, in 1930, an engineer and a doctor at Harvard University devised a contraption familiarly known as the "iron lung" to provide them with artificial respiration. Paralyzed patients were encased in a horizontal metal chamber the size of a large refrigerator, with the head poking out through a snug-fitting collar. Inside, the air pressure was made to rise and fall at a rate approximately that of normal breathing. This caused the chest to expand and contract rhythmically, filling and compressing the lungs as it did so. For those who survived the disease, imprisonment in the iron lung usually lasted a matter of weeks; others never recovered their ability to breathe sufficiently to leave and were destined to spend the rest of their lives inside. Clumsy as the breathing devices were, they provided enough support to critical organs to make the difference between life and death.

Thanks to vaccines, polio is scarcely remembered today, but mechanical descendants of the first artificial respirator are still used in the form of high-tech ventilators, and tens of thousands of people with compromised lungs depend on them. Some of the devices are small enough to be carried around like a shoulder bag so that their users are no longer confined at home but are free to travel and work in the community.

spark of life

Repairing or adjusting heart rhythms through artificial means was another area of interest to medical inventors. Normal human heart rhythm is extremely variable, so imitating it was bound to be tricky. At rest, the healthy heart contracts and expands on an average of 72 times per minute, but during sleep it pumps more slowly. Under physical or emotional stress—running a race, watching a horror movie, having a high fever—it may rise to as many as 200 beats per minute. Controlling the beat is the task of the sino-atrial node, a cluster of specialized cells located on top of the right atrium of the heart.

The cells of this tiny natural "pacemaker" transmit faint electrical impulses to the nerve cells to power the heart muscle. Disturbances in these electrical impulses, which can be tracked as a wavy up-and-down line on an electrocardiograph (EKG), result in chronic slow, fast, or irregular heart beats (arrhythmias). Arrhythmias can have moderately serious consequences to health, including dizziness, palpitations, and breathing difficulties. Ultimately, they can cause heart failure, when blood pumping becomes so inefficient that the heart is over-whelmed and stops altogether. Though the precise work-ings of the heart have only been recently understood, scientists have long suspected that electricity had curious effects on muscle tissue, and even suggested that elec-tricity might be the essential "spark of life." Some experi-mented with electroresuscitation. The tale of "Frankenstein's monster," originating in 1818, tells of a robotlike creature whose parts are "brought together and endued with vital warmth" through the application of electricity. But in reality, electrical stimulation to the body failed to find significant practical use other than mildly warming it.

Then, in the 1950s, two Minnesotans—pioneer heart surgeon C. Walton Lillehei and graduate electrical engi-neering student Earl Bakken—devised a table-size machine capable of providing rhythmic electrical impulses to the heart. This primitive "pacemaker" deliv-ered the pulses via electrodes that were implanted in the patient's chest, so that there was always a danger of skin burns. And it had to be plugged into household current,

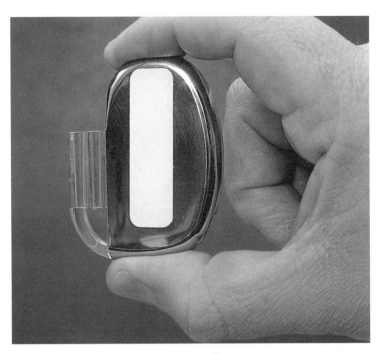

A pacemaker

which left patients who were dependent on it little room to maneuver, particularly during an occasional power outage. Nevertheless, physicians concerned with improving the health of heart patients were quick to recognize that Lillehei and Bakken were onto something.

In 1957, a decade after the first miniaturized semiconductor transistor was invented at Bell Labs, the surgeon and the young engineer proudly unveiled the first wearable, external battery-powered heart pacemaker.[7] About the size of a paperback book, the scaled-down pacemaker could be worn inconspicuously on the belt. It heralded an array of powerful new techniques for correcting chronic breakdowns in body parts and systems. Today, more than 130,000 Americans are outfitted yearly with artificial pacemakers, now so tiny and compact that the entire mechanism weighs less than an ounce and can be implanted under the skin with wires to the heart. Unlike the first pacemaker, which had a single beat, the newer implants have programming capability with sensors that detect the need for faster and slower rates as the body places different demands on the heart. Telemetry—by which a technician far away can check and adjust the pacemaker when a patient holds the device up to the telephone—was introduced in the 1980s; this bit of wizardry provides an additional convenience and safeguard for people who depend on pacemakers.

At the same time that Bakken and Lillehei were putting the finishing touches on their first invention, a second major breakthrough involving the medical uses of electricity was made in a laboratory at Johns Hopkins Medical Center in Baltimore, Maryland. There, William Kouwenhoven was working on an assignment from the Edison Electric Institute of New York. The company needed a tool to resuscitate electrical workers whose hearts were accidentally shocked into stopping when they were working around power lines. Kouwenhoven's solution, unveiled in 1957, was the forerunner of the defibrillators and electrical paddles used to treat cardiac arrest in hospital emergency and operating rooms today. Defibrillators have also been placed on airplanes and in police and emergency rescue vehicles.

Kouwenhoven's device is also the grandfather of the implantable defibrillator, a million times more powerful than a pacemaker, that patients with a chronically unreliable heartbeat can wear within their chests. Programmed to recognize the symptoms of cardiac arrest, the defibrillator automatically shocks the heart back into action on those life-threatening occasions when it stops beating altogether. The jolt, which has been compared to being kicked in the chest by a horse, really works. The U.S. Food and Drug Administration, in granting approval to the device in 1985, found that among the patient population with certain types of uncontrolled heart-rhythm defects, the death rate due to cardiac arrest fell from as high as 66 percent to 5 percent![8]

whole-hearted efforts

Important as the valves and pacemakers and defibrillators were, they could not solve every heart problem. Whether because of birth defects, or injury or disease sustained later, some hearts simply cannot be made good enough to keep their owners alive and functioning. For these people, the choice of last resort focused on heart transplantation.

In December 1967 the world was stunned when South Africa's Dr. Christiaan Barnard transplanted the heart of a young woman killed in a car accident into the chest cavity of Louis Washkansky. The 55-year-old Cape Town grocer had suffered several heart attacks and had been given only a few weeks to live, making him a candidate for desperate measures. Unlike kidney transplants, which had been scarcely noticed by the general public, the idea of heart transplantation seized the public's imagination. When initial reports of the outcome were positive, the feat was compared in its boldness to man's attempts to reach the moon. Doctors everywhere hailed it as the beginning of a new era in medicine, and within a few days 65 other surgical teams in 22 countries replicated Barnard's unprecedented surgery. But the public soon learned that heart transplantation was still a risky business. Louis Washkansky's donated heart beat only 18 days before he and the organ gave out.

Results everywhere else were also discouraging. Five years after the dawning of human heart transplantation, only one of the 101 patients given this new lease on life was still alive. (This was, after all, happening a decade before immunosuppressants like cyclosporine were

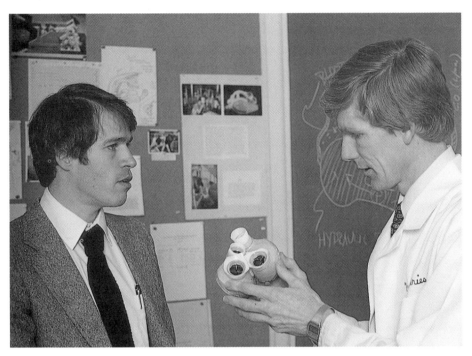

Robert Jarvik, left, who designed the first permanent artificial heart in 1981, and Dr. William DeVries, who implanted the device in patient Barney Clark.

developed, and the majority of the failures were ultimately due to organ rejection.) For the next two decades, heart transplants were performed only infrequently and with scarcely better outcomes. Improved results with transplanted human hearts came only with the advent of immunosuppressants in the 1980s. Today, as many as 3,500 heart transplants are performed annually around the world with the one-year survival rate running an impressive 90 percent or better. Many recipients do very well indeed: One of Dr. Barnard's later patients lived 23 years before dying of unrelated causes.

Meanwhile, another approach to heart malfunction came under intense study: the substitution of an entirely artificial heart. To understand the complexity of this task, consider what work the artificial heart must duplicate. In circulating oxygen and nutrients throughout the body, the average adult heart must pump five quarts of blood per minute without stopping over the course of a lifetime, which can be as long as 100 years or more. Looked at even conservatively, the average heart probably beats more than 2.5 billion times, at variable rates that adjust to the various activities the body is engaged in. A fully satisfactory artificial version of the human pump would have to be superbly engineered of the finest materials and equipped with extremely versatile controls. Perhaps comparisons with moon rocketry were not so far-fetched after all.

Denton Cooley and Domingo Liotta of Houston, Texas, were the first surgeons to implant a completely artificial heart, in 1969. But this somewhat primitive device was intended not as a permanent replacement but rather as a temporary substitute while a human donor heart was found; unfortunately, the temporary failed almost immediately. Still, the idea remained valid, and doctors and engineers continued to work on finding better solutions. Eventually, after 20 years of experiment, Utah bioengineer Robert Jarvik thought he had a workable model for a permanent heart, and in 1982 he persuaded heart surgeon William DeVries of the University of Utah Medical Center in Salt Lake City to give his device a try. In a seven and a half hour operation, the so-called Jarvik-7 was implanted in the chest of Barney Clark, a 61-year-old retired dentist, who because of his age was not considered a suitable candidate for a precious human heart transplant.

With its polyurethane and aluminum internal mechanism and external support from 375 pounds of air compressor and other machinery, the Jarvik-7 did seem to revive Clark's prospects for a time. But less than four months later the dentist was dead, the victim of various complications including circulatory collapse. Dr. Jarvik and others went back to the drawing boards to devise improved versions of the mechanical heart, but they proved useful only as stopgap measures while patients waited for the real thing. In 1990 the Food and Drug Administration banned their further use in humans until they could be made substantially more reliable. The concept seems certain to be realized, however. As the number of people suffering from irreversible heart disease continues to rise and the supply of suitable human organs for transplantation falls ever shorter, the pressure to devise alternative sources in the form of artificial organs can only increase.

Blood

The formal introduction of one person's blood into another's for the purpose of restoring blood lost to disease or accidental hemorrhage is a little over a century old, but cruder forms of transfusion go far back in history.

In Ancient Egypt, the blood of ducks, geese, pigeons, goats, sheep, and cattle were prescribed for a variety of conditions. The Romans believed that swallowing fresh human blood had a salutary effect, and blood spilled by a gladiator in the ring was a specific for epilepsy. Blood from a freshly killed lion, an animal known for its valor, was also said to be a good preparation for going into battle. Similar ideas persist today in the folklore of many cultures.

A far more common practice relating to the role of blood in healing in centuries past was the "therapeutic bleeding" of patients for whatever ailed them. Bleeding was generally the responsibility of barber-surgeons, who cut open veins to relieve what was believed to be excessive pressure or heat, and of physicians, who applied blood-sucking leeches to draw off blood. As if to interject a degree of scientific legitimacy to this act, the barbers and surgeons often carried out their odd rituals according to "bleeding calendars," illustrated charts that listed optimal days and body sites according to the position of the moon and stars.

Not until 1628 did the transfusing of blood between living organisms become a practical reality. That was the year in which English physician William Harvey proposed a workable theory for the circulation of blood within the body's closed system of arteries, veins, and heart. But as no one knew that such exchanges could only work reliably between compatible human blood types, blood donation continued to be an uncertain method of therapy. Doctors routinely used sheep blood, in ready supply, to treat their sickly human patients, and when the patients took a turn for the worse, they presumed that the disease rather than the blood was at fault.

Practices in transfusing blood improved considerably in the mid-nineteenth century, thanks to the invention of a hypodermic syringe with a hollow needle. Battlefield transfusions were first performed a quarter century later, during the Franco-Prussian War.

With increased use of transfusions, physicians observed that humans sometimes suffered a severe reaction to foreign blood. Sometimes the cause was thought to be clotting, but a more fundamental problem—that there were distinct human blood types—was not discovered until 1901 when the Austrian-born American scientist Karl Landsteiner identified conclusively that there were distinct blood components, known as antigens and antibodies. Landsteiner went on to explain the mechanism by which the body's immune system sifts through the components, accepting blood that is like its own but rejecting blood that is different. He eventually developed the ABO blood classification system by which all blood is "typed" today.

Meanwhile, a practical anticoagulant was found, making it possible to store blood for brief periods of time. By World War I it became the practice to collect blood from donors gathered at one location and transfuse it later into the wounded, even at a battlefield first-aid station. That development led to the idea of the civilian "blood bank," the first of which was opened in Chicago in 1937. World War II brought still further strides as scientists learned to separate blood into a number of useful elements, such as plasma and clotting factors, paving the way for battlefield miracles and peacetime improvements in the lives of hemophiliacs. (The Germans and the Japanese during these years were so engrossed in the notion of "racial purity" that they lagged well behind the Allies in transfusion science until late in the war.)

Though some commercial facilities exist in which people can donate blood in exchange for money, the larger share of blood used in health facilities is gathered free from volunteers, typically at blood banks operated by the American Red Cross. Blood donation is a quick, almost painless procedure. People wishing to give blood are first screened to ensure that they are not anemic. Those who pass then present an arm to a technician, who inserts a small hollow needle into an artery and collects about a pint of blood as it drips steadily into a sanitary bag nearby. The donor may feel a temporary sensation of light-headedness but is able to leave within minutes. Since a healthy adult normally has 10 to 12 pints of blood in the system and lost blood is naturally replaced within a few weeks, it is not uncommon for donors to give several times a year without adverse effects. The donated blood is typed, tested for the presence of any undesirable substances such as hepatitis or the HIV virus that might infect the recipient, and processed for a variety of medical uses. It can then be chilled and stored for up to four weeks.

While whole blood was commonly used in transfusions until the 1980s, today blood is separated into various components such as packed red blood cells (for leukemia), albumin (for burn victims), clotting factor (for hemophiliacs), and plasma (the watery remainder fluid containing dissolved proteins, fats, glucose and salts). Maintaining adequate supplies of all kinds of blood and blood constituents is difficult, particularly in times of public-health emergencies when demand is especially high, so scientists have been working for some time to find artificial blood substitutes. The first such products are now available. One situation where it may prove particularly useful is in treating patients who, for religious reasons, decline to use human blood products. All told, donated blood saves tens of thousands of lives each year, including victims of serious accidents as well as surgical patients and people being treated for chronic anemia, cancer, bleeding ulcers, leukemia, hemophilia, and other severe illnesses.

One of the makers of artificial human blood has introduced the first artificial blood product for dogs. As blood banks for animals are scarce, this is an important development for veterinary medicine, as well.

4 YOU NEED IT?
WE GOT IT—MAYBE

The story of artificial arms and legs, of pacemakers and transplants, is first and foremost a story of medical and technical developments. But it is also a story of changes in human attitudes and social policy. As noted in earlier chapters, the public has gradually come to recognize the extent of the practical and economic barriers faced by the physically handicapped. People now believe that government has a responsibility, directly or indirectly, to lower those barriers and to help those with disabilities—a sizable segment of the population—realize a better quality of life.

Bolstering the state workers compensation laws introduced in the first two decades of the twentieth century, the federal government organized the Vocational Rehabilitation Act in 1920, which included provisions for retraining injured workers in alternative trades and skills. These laws were further expanded in the 1930s to include a host of rehabilitation services for other categories of the disabled. And in 1978 still larger commitments to the disabled were made when the National Institutes of

Health created the forerunner of the National Institute on Disability and Rehabilitation Research with its own sizable research budget. On another front, the civil rights of the disabled were formally recognized and protected with the enactment of the landmark Americans With Disabilities Act in 1990.

We see the beneficial results of these progressive changes in such obvious things as handicap-accessible entrances to public buildings and ramped curbs on the corners of city intersections, and in laws prohibiting discrimination in housing and in the workplace. But there are many less obvious advances in the way American society recognizes the rights and needs of the disabled—special vocational training, subsidies for some kinds of prosthetic and orthotic aids, and government research grants to help scientists, engineers, and specialists in rehabilitation medicine continue to search for better solutions to the unique physical problems that some members of our community face every day.

We see it also in the growing importance of recreational and social programs for the disabled. The next time you watch or read about one of the major marathon races that take place each year in U.S. cities, notice the numbers of disabled who participate. The 1997 New York City Marathon, for example, included 260 competitors from the Achilles Track Club, an association of disabled athletes.

The first Olympic-style games for disabled athletes was organized in Rome in 1960. Limited to wheel-chair competitors with spinal-cord injuries, the games have since been expanded to include competitive international games for the blind, for amputees, and for individuals with cerebral palsy. By 1996 when Atlanta, Georgia, hosted the Paralympics, as they are now known, more than 3,500 competitors from 120 countries participated in 17 different sports. These events, which feature supe-

Sprinter Tony Volpentest, born without hands or feet, won both the 100-meter and 200-meter races at the 1996 Paralympics with the help of high performance prostheses.

rior competitors by any standard, showcase what can be done with rehabilitation training, a "can-do" attitude, and state-of-the-art prosthetics and orthotics. Coincidentally, they provide inspiration to millions of disabled and nondisabled to do more in their own lives.

The change in social attitudes and expectations also led to the creation of many private support organizations to assist the disabled. The first organization dedicated to rehabilitation, the Cleveland Rehabilitation Center, was founded in Ohio in 1899. This was followed in 1917 by the Red Cross Institute for the Crippled and Disabled in New York and by various privately supported schools for crippled children. Groups like the American Heart Association, the National Kidney Foundation, the Paralyzed Veterans, the Disabled American Veterans, Shriners Hospitals, and scores of other national fund-raising and informational groups also formed in the years after World War I. But perhaps no private organization has been more influential in changing public attitudes about disabilities and society's responsibilities than the National Foundation for Infantile Paralysis (NFIP).

Through the NFIP's "March of Dimes" fund, begun in the 1930s, tens of millions of Americans have contributed, often one dime at a time, to the treatment and rehabilitation of children and young adults with disabilities. The driving force behind the March of Dimes was Franklin D. Roosevelt, the thirty-second president. Roosevelt had contracted polio in 1921 when he was 39 years old. Fortunate in coming from a family of wealth and influence, he had received the best of care, including what was then state-of-the-art physical therapy and braces for his paralyzed legs. Though he would remain paralyzed in the lower half of his body, Roosevelt was eventually able to return to active life, but he knew well that millions of others had little help available. Through his charismatic leadership, the NFIP raised money to bring millions of disabled people the iron lungs (external breathing machines), orthotics, and rehabilitation they desperately needed.

The NFIP also channeled funds into scholarships to train hundreds of new physical and occupational therapists. It also invested extensively in medical research, which led not only to better knowledge of how to treat paralyses of all kinds but also supported work in the development of vaccines. In 1954 the first preventive vaccine was successfully tested, and within a couple of years new polio cases fell from close to 60,000 a year to almost none.

the body electric

Meanwhile, great advances were also being made in the treatment of amputees and the design of their prostheses. World War II, with its large numbers of returning wounded, provided a powerful incentive. Amputees reasonably argued that with so much progress in so many other areas of technology, they deserved better than the still heavy, awkward hardware they were getting. A lot of other people thought so too. A major conference of doctors and business leaders was called, and funding was found to help a dozen of the nation's best medical schools set up model programs to teach and carry out research in the new medical specialty called rehabilitation medicine. The makers of prosthetics and orthotics also decided to create professional standards for themselves.

Beginning in 1948, prosthetists had to have a college degree, advanced training in orthotics and prosthetics, and on-the-job experience before gaining professional certification. No longer could an individual open a workshop in the back of a garage and hang out a sign claiming to know what he or she was doing and hope to have clients in need of an arm or leg show up. At the same time Dr. Norman Kirk, surgeon general of the U. S. Army, asked the National Academy of Sciences for advice and help on developing new and better prosthetics. Early in 1945 the National Academy enlisted physicians, surgeons, and engineers at sixteen of the nation's leading universities to take up the problem. They also sought the help of a few bright minds in industry, where wartime activities were giving way to more peaceful pursuits.

Teams made up of medical researchers, physical therapists, and engineers focused on analyzing the way healthy normal arms and legs, hands and feet, actually operate—thus laying the foundations for the twin disciplines of biomechanics and biophysics. The premise was that good artificial limbs could not be invented without first knowing precisely what actions they were supposed to imitate and what tasks they had to carry out. Researchers at the University of California at Berkeley, who were given responsibility for lower-limb study, examined what happens, for example, when a person walks. Gait had been studied earlier, of course, but now it was approached at a more scientific level. Using all sorts of precise diagnostic instruments, they sought to discover how the body's weight is distributed, how long the normal stride is in persons of different ages and heights and energy levels. Researchers at the University of California at Los Angeles did much the same kinds of studies for upper limbs. Still other groups went to work at the New York University Institute for Rehabilitation Medicine, at the Army Prosthetic Research Laboratory at Walter Reed Hospital, Washington, D.C., and at the Navy's Prosthetics Research Center near Oakland, California.

In what would become a pattern for many kinds of government-sponsored research, the information gathered at one center was supposed to be shared with all the other centers where different phases of investigation were under way. Knowing more about the normal movements of arms and legs was an important beginning to better prostheses and orthoses, for sure. But postwar limb designers also needed to learn more about how the underlying skeletal muscles and nerves normally work together to produce those movements. As indicated in the preceding chapter, scientists had discovered centuries earlier that electrical impulses were somehow involved in movement. In 1744, Johannes Kruger at the University of Halle in Germany went so far as to speculate that a paralyzed muscle might someday be restored to action by electrical shocks.[1] Benjamin Franklin used static electricity experimentally to treat paralysis, and other free-thinking scientists tried everything from primitive generators to electric eels to stimulate muscles.

The notion that natural movement is actually brought about when electrical impulses travel through nerve fibers to bundles of muscle fibers is a relatively recent discovery. These so-called myoelectric impulses, generated by chemical reactions in the body, cause the muscles to become irritated. Irritation, in turn, causes them to contract, or tighten up, moving the bones to which they are connected in certain predictable ways.

feedback and muscle memory

Also relatively recent is the discovery that the electrical messages are themselves triggered by different kinds of nerve endings that detect heat, cold, pain, and spatial position. The nerve endings are linked to a network that reaches all the way from the tips of the toes and fingers to the brain and back again; their messages are processed automatically in the brain where "feedback" mechanisms "tell" the muscles what to do. They selectively moderate what the muscle groups do in order to keep us walking upright, avoiding contact with surfaces that are too hot or cold, reaching for things with just the right amount of force, and flexing with just the right degree of direction.

86

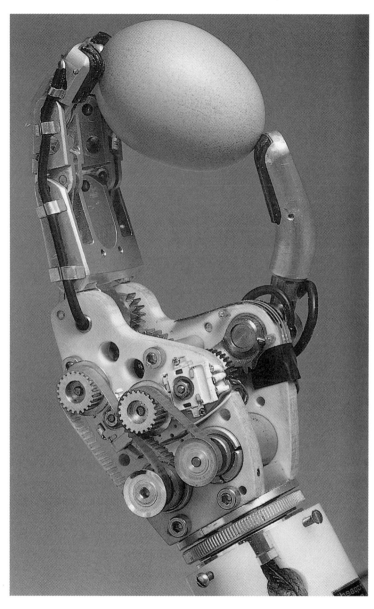

This lightweight myoelectric hand is teamed with delicate sensors on the wearer's forearm and a built-in computer to perform an array of delicate movements when the individual flexes existing muscles.

We rarely give conscious thought to how we move. Rather, we learn through practice what we need to do to achieve each movement, and we retain the skill as "muscle memory" for the rest of our lives—unless, of course, something happens to make us forget (a paralytic stroke) or to make us move differently (an injury, including amputation).

The results are movements of almost indescribable complexity and subtlety. Think, for example, of the fine motor adjustments of the hands and fingers required to operate a computer keyboard or sew a fine seam; or of the legs and feet to maneuver a soccer ball through a tiny opening in the defense. Sometimes the movements must be relatively simple but powerful, like swinging a hammer or climbing a step.

The new generation of prosthetists and rehabilitation specialists hoped to go Dr. Giuliano Vanghetti one better by finding ways to link amputees' remaining myoelectric capabilities and muscle memories to artificial arms and legs. Tall as that order seemed, it was already being investigated by scientists and engineers involved in another postwar enterprise, that of industrial robotics, or as it is known scientifically, *bionics*. Bionics is a modern word that combines the idea of biology and electronics. While the so-called Bionic Man and Bionic Woman are pure movie fantasy, they are loosely based on notions that are real enough nowadays, namely that machines can be programmed by computers to "think." "Smart machines" can, in fact, move and manipulate objects in response to changes in the immediate environment, much as humans are equipped to do. This is markedly different from simple automation, where machines do the same repetitive task over and over.

The first practical robot, developed in the early 1950s, was a stand-alone jointed robotic arm and hand. Used to move dangerous materials in a U.S. nuclear power plant, the robotic arm took information about its surroundings to adjust its movements, just as a human arm uses "feedback" from its sense of touch, determining heat and position to make its own corrections and adjustments. So successful were the early robotic devices in doing certain dangerous, unpleasant, and monotonous tasks, that they were gradually adapted to perform many other kinds of work, from spot welding and painting to assembling automobiles. It would be only a matter of time, the prosthetics researchers knew, before the techniques used in robotics design could be applied to designing artificial limbs for humans.

working out the kinks

Research teams at the National Academy of Sciences (later transferred to the Veterans Administration) concentrated on four areas of scientific investigation—limb movements, socket design and suspension, prostheses materials, and methods of prostheses manufacture. Each team was supported by an array of newly developed measuring and analytical tools. And each team was free to borrow ideas from any and every discipline where they saw something of relevance to their own research.

In this way, limb movement researchers could employ the newest improvements in motion-picture cameras and in neuromuscular sensing equipment to analyze normal movements. (It was found, for example, that the human arm is capable of 27 different motions.) At the same time, surgically trained investigators were looking more closely at amputation surgery, wondering whether techniques might be improved to better prepare amputees for the prostheses they would eventually use. It soon became obvious that some kinds of surgical procedures were better than others in determining how the body healed afterward and in how they distributed the body's weight within the limb to create the fewest pressure points.

89

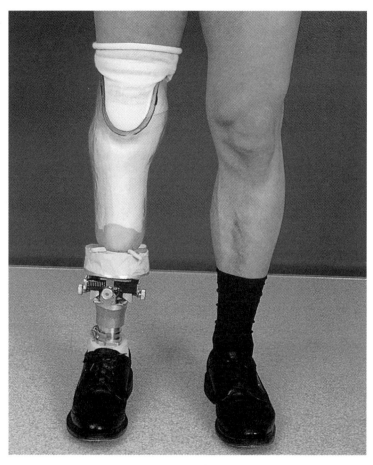

This sophisticated artificial leg and foot has screws above the ankle to adjust the shock absorption for the wearer's weight and stride.

Research in biomechanics showed, for example, that a quadrilateral (squarish) stump and socket provide more support and comfort to the amputee than the traditional circular stump and "plug-fit" socket.

As for materials, the wood and leather upon which the prosthetists had depended for so many centuries no longer seemed satisfactory. Wood requires individual carving and shaping, costly and time-consuming techniques that depend on the talents and experience of a master craftsman every time; leather, while easier to work with, absorbs perspiration and is hard to keep clean and supple over many months and years. Both combine to make a heavy appliance that tires the wearer and discourages activity.

To overcome the deficiencies of these and other materials, engineers at Northrop Aviation, which had been one of the leading designers and manufacturers of lightweight fighter planes in World War II, came up with new composite metals that were lighter and more durable, particularly when subjected to the physically active lives that postwar amputees were determined to adopt. Northrop engineers also introduced thermosetting plastics to make transparent custom-fit molded sockets. This advance permitted the prosthetist to peer inside "where the rubber meets the road," as one prosthetist put it, to see precisely how well stumps and their support sockets matched.[2]

The resulting precision fit was also important in holding the prosthesis on. Up to World War II, amputees had to wear over-the-shoulder suspenders or waist belt-suspenders for stability. Now, with nearly perfect contact, many prostheses could be held in place by suction fit, much in the way that dentures stay put.

The newer leg prostheses were redesigned to provide greater stability and mobility for different kinds of wearers too. Some appliances for above-the-knee amputees featured a constant-friction knee with an adjustable brake that made it possible to tune the swing of the lower leg to a fairly consistent walking speed; this made the artificial legs reasonably well-suited to older patients whose movements are fairly restricted and predictable. But younger, more active amputees needed something more versatile to fit their lifestyles. These improvements were eventually found in knee systems that featured hydraulic shock absorbers. In essence, a tiny piston drives hydraulic fluid through a small hole in the cylinder to create variable degrees of resistance; the faster one walks, or even runs, the greater the potential shock to the residual limb and the more shock absorption provided by the hydraulic knee. New foot designs that offered better cushioning, shock-absorption, and flexibility in rough terrain were also developed.

As the public became more used to seeing amputees out and about, and as the internal mechanisms of artificial legs became more complex, the outward appearance of artificial limbs also changed. Traditional legs had been made to look as much like the natural leg as possible, but amputees paid a price in having a leg that weighed more and moved less easily. Now something reminiscent of the old peg legs was reintroduced, only this time instead of a wooden peg it was a steel and aluminum pylon with a foot on the end. The pylon (or endoskeleton, as prosthetists describe this kind of open framework) could be adjusted in length to allow for a young person's continuing growth. Its interior spaces were filled with all sorts of visible working components like shock absorbers and springs that could be readily serviced. Wearers could still get a foam cover for their pylon if they cared about appearance, but the real interest now was in function and comfort rather than form.

Much effort was devoted to learning more about the unique physical demands that having an amputated limb puts on a person and how rehabilitation training could help. For example, it was discovered, through studies in physiology laboratories, that amputees consume on average considerably more oxygen than the rest of us to perform comparable tasks. The reasons are many, but they include the fact that an amputee must summon extra energy to deal with the passive or "dead weight" of the artificial limb together with the loss of "live lift," the barely noticed but substantial springiness that comes from muscle reflexes when you take a step. The more of the limb that is amputated, the greater the effort required.

For example, a person with an above-the-knee amputation will consume about 65 percent more oxygen than his able-bodied friend doing the same activity; a person with a below-the-knee amputation burns closer to 10 percent more oxygen. While breathing faster and doing aerobic exercises to develop greater lung capacity can help the amputee meet the greater energy demands, the more practical long-term solution for many older amputees is to become mentally and practically attuned to walking comfortably at a reduced speed. Younger amputees, however, often amaze their doctors and everyone around them by developing extraordinary aerobic capacities, enough to make them stand out in the sports they choose to play.

arms race

Arms and hands presented a somewhat different set of challenges. Post–World War II design teams looked at three different options. In the simplest version, an artificial arm could be, like the "Sunday arms" of old, supplied to serve appearances only. Such an arm would be a lightweight, passive device that restored symmetry and appearance to the body. It would also have the advantage of being relatively cheap to manufacture and maintain, requiring little upkeep or adjustment because it had so few moving parts. Some amputees whose other hand served them well enough found this solution satisfactory for their purposes. The second option, desirable for individuals who wanted to be able to perform simple gripping and lifting actions, was a body-powered arm and hand.

Many variations on this idea were produced beginning in the late 1940s, and they continue to be used especially by older amputees. Using a concept borrowed from puppetry, the body-powered arm relies on motion transferred from the opposite shoulder to the artificial hand or a hook via strap, cable, and pulleys. A shrug of the able-bodied shoulder causes the distant mechanical "hand" to open and its spring-loaded fingers to pull apart; another shrug causes the springs to release and the hand to close again. But mastering the equipment requires a lot of concentration, and the resulting movements remain relatively crude.

The third option, which excited postwar designers the most, was to create a myoelectric arm. Taking up where Dr. Vanghetti and his kineplastic hand had ultimately failed early in the twentieth century, and borrowing from ideas in play among designers of industrial robots, researchers at IBM and other overseas centers sought to design an arm that was almost human. They soon discovered, however, that while the small electrical charges that travel back and forth to the brain via the nerves are sufficient to operate an extremely efficient natural arm and hand, they are not strong enough to operate power-hungry artificial parts. (It was rather like trying to light up a room with the glow of a jarful of lightning bugs.) What was needed were electric motors to power the work.

The motors had to be small enough and smart enough to tell prosthetic hands not only when to open and close and prosthetic wrists when to rotate—all fairly simple "on-off" instructions—but also by how much, how far, and how fast in each situation. These actions take brainlike subconscious thinking and required tiny electrodes, microprocessors, minute circuitry, and rechargeable batteries, all recent developments. The first myoelectric arms were brought out in the 1970s. Though they were strictly experimental and too expensive and

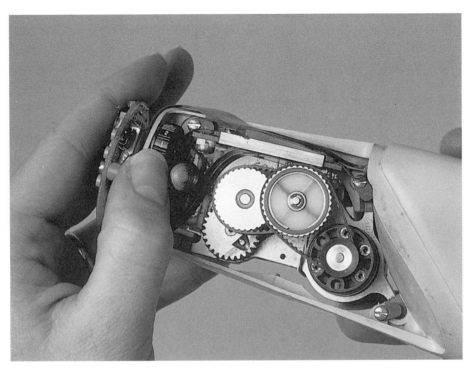

The inner workings of an artificial hand

unreliable to be used by the majority of people who might benefit from them, they worked well enough to give everyone involved confidence in the future.

Reid Hilton, a young Californian, was selected as one of the first recipients of the new technology.[3] Hilton had lost his right arm below the elbow in an accident; his still functional upper arm was surgically implanted with electrodes placed over the two principal nerves; wires were led from the electrodes to a power pack on his belt. The pack included a signal booster and a motor to carry out the movements. A third electrode was set up as a ground to protect Hilton against electrical shocks. With this rig, the young man was able to initiate movements by merely thinking of them; the nerve impulses that began as thoughts in his brain traveled along familiar and undamaged routes to the nerve fibers in his upper arm muscles. When they reached the area of the sensors, their signals were picked up and carried along wires to the waist pack where they were amplified and used to control the motors that actually moved the joints and fingers. With practice, Hilton learned to grasp delicate objects, open a jar, button his jacket, tie his shoes, and grip a handle with a force of up to 40 pounds (18 kg). Remarkably, Reid's grip exceeded the strength of most ordinary people, who make do with 25 pounds (11 kg) of force.

Myoelectric prostheses are still in their adolescence in terms of technical proficiency. Nevertheless, some prostheses are so finely tuned that they can sense when a coffee cup is beginning to slip in the hand and feed information back to the muscles to increase the fingers' grip just enough to steady the cup but not so much as to crack it! Activity-specific hands are also available, with custom adaptations for basketball, fishing, baseball, golf, and various job-related skills.

Just on the horizon are appliances that detect sensations of hot and cold and texture in their artificial parts. These futurist appliances will work their marvels, say the bioengineers, with a mosaic of artificial sensors scattered across their prosthetic fingers, much as sensory nerves in the natural hand. The artificial sensors will pick up raw information (heat, for example), encode the information into distinct electrical patterns on a microprocessor within, and send the patterns by wireless radio signals to receivers in the residual upper arm. From there, the information will be delivered to nerve fibers, fed back to the brain for interpretation, and the muscles will be stimulated to react appropriately with nearly the speed of natural reflexes.

If scientists can do something as delicate as restoring nerve communication between an artificial hand and brain, and if they can reattach fingers sliced off in accidents, why can't they transplant a donor hand where one is missing? They can—at least in some circumstances. In a surgical first, a team of doctors in Lyons, France, performed this remarkable feat in September 1998.[4] Working with Clint Hallam, an Australian whose forearm and hand had been severed some 14 years earlier, they attached a donor arm taken from a suitable cadaver. The delicate operation, which involved experts in microsurgery, orthopedics, and transplant surgery, took nearly 14 hours to complete. Not only were bones and flesh connected, but hundreds of complementary arteries, veins, muscles, tendons and nerves had to be stitched together end to end.

No sooner were the reports of the French surgery released than it was revealed that a team in Louisville, Kentucky, had been practicing for months to perform a similar surgical experiment, just waiting for the right set of circumstances to come along. In January 1999 they got their wish. Matthew David Scott, a New Jersey man who had lost his hand and wrist in a fireworks accident years before, volunteered and was given a donor hand.[5] At this writing, it is still too early to pronounce either surgery wholly successful—the danger period for graft-host rejections in this kind of surgery can last many months—but all indications have been positive. Both men report that sensation—the characteristic most difficult to restore after severe trauma—is returning to the fingers, and muscles powered by the ulnar nerve, which serves the little finger, are starting to function.

one step at a time

Given the tremendous advances that prosthetic engineers and medical scientists have made on behalf of amputees, it is not surprising that much investigational work has also been done in the field of orthotics. In the period immediately after World War II an unusually large group of paralyzed veterans and polio survivors needed to be served. Even with dramatic improvements in the medical treatment of trauma, there are thousands of paralyzed survivors of spinal cord injuries. The National Spinal Cord Injury Association estimates that annually between 7,800 and 13,000 injuries resulting in paralysis occur in the United States. Most are associated with car and motorcycle accidents, and most involve young adults.

While orthotics have many points in common with prosthetics, orthotics present unique and challenging problems of their own. Whereas modern prostheses are designed to be hollow and can be equipped with a lot of interior electrical wiring and hardware without adding bulk, orthoses have to be applied over existing but non-functioning parts of the body. Everything that goes to making a brace strong and rigid and to aiding the paralyzed person to be erect and to move is therefore "extra." The extra weight and extra bulk inevitably place another big burden on a body that is already weakened. And every paralysis, every twisted body is different, requiring different solutions. So while prosthetics design moved ahead rather smartly in the decades following World War II, it has taken somewhat longer for orthotics design to go high tech.

Today's braces are considerably more comfortable and lighter in weight than the massive braces that, for example, President Roosevelt had to rely on. Physical therapy methods have also come a long way toward helping people disabled by musculoskeletal problems to enjoy greater mobility. However, for paralyzed people the search for ways to restore muscle function and overcome paralysis is of paramount importance. Fortunately, researchers have begun to make some genuine progress in that area.

To understand what they are hoping to accomplish, you first need to understand what causes paralysis. Paralysis results from breaks in the nerve network that enables messages of all kinds to flow between the brain and muscles. A network break may be rooted in the brain (stroke, cerebral palsy, brain injury, for example), in a muscle disorder (muscular dystrophy), or in the spinal cord and its major branches (polio, multiple sclerosis, or spinal cord injury). The injured body may look normal enough on the outside, but inside there is a gap in some area of the nerve transmission line; the result is that essential messages can't get through.

The spinal cord is particularly vulnerable to accidental injury. The spinal cord consists of tens of thousands of delicate white cords, actually nerve fibers, that are all bunched together at the source—the brain itself. From there, the fibers extend downward in a two-way main transmission line that is protected only by the stacked column of separate vertebrae known as the backbone. Nerve fibers communicating with each part of the body emerge like branches through dozens of sideways open- ings in the vertebral column. A sharp blow, a wrenching twist, a penetrating wound in the region of the backbone, or a fall leading to compression of any of the vertebrae, can snap or cut or crush the spinal cord. The higher on the column the damage occurs, the more extensive the paralysis, because no signals can come or go beyond that interruption.

A victim of this kind of injury is Christopher Reeve, the well-known actor. In 1995, Reeve was thrown headfirst from his horse during a jumping competition. He frac- tured the first two cervical vertebrae in his neck and crushed his spinal cord at the point where it exits from the skull. As a result of this injury, referred to in medical shorthand as a C-2, Reeve became a quadriplegic, with paralysis in virtually every part of his body below the neck.

For the moment, the short-term goal for people like Reeve is to maintain the best possible muscle tone that physical therapy can provide and wait, hoping that researchers will someday find the means to repair the broken connections. One approach under investigation in several research centers is to bathe the area of spinal cord injury with the same specialized proteins found in still-developing fetal spinal cords and brains. The theory is that this procedure may somehow trick the nerve cells there into growing new connections in the same way that fetal spinal cords do.[6] Scientists have already accomplished nerve regeneration in experimental mice and guinea pigs, which indicates that the principle is valid.

Meanwhile, there is a technology known as Functional Electrical Stimulation, or FES, and for paraplegics like 15-year-old Robert Fey, it's already providing the means for movement. Basically, FES technology uses much of the same science involved in myoelectric prostheses, only this time it uses electricity to stimulate and control the body's own paralyzed muscles rather than to control artificial limbs. Going back to the experiments of Benjamin Franklin and others, modern-day medical researchers have devised in FES technology the equivalent of a prosthesis for the nerves. FES achieves this feat with a system of electrodes, nickel-cadmium batteries, plus computer and control switch. As the FES computer is a fairly sophisticated device, it can be pre-programmed to send its radio signals to the electrodes in a particular sequence that simulates the sequence found in normal movement. The nerves and the muscles, which make no distinction between normal and artificially generated messages, do their thing, and something like normal movement results.

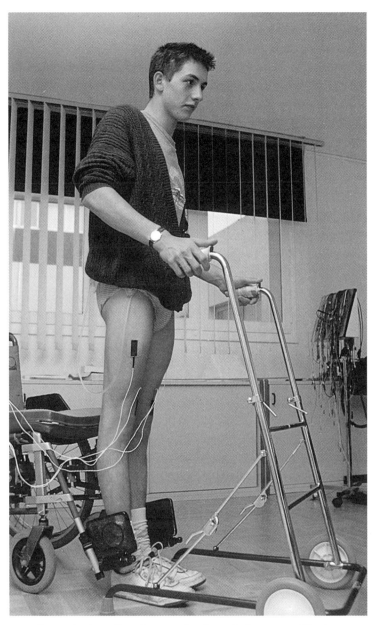

Paraplegics often have spinal cord damage affecting the nerve roots. Here, electrodes over relevant muscles help a patient to stand and walk.

Fey, who can now stand and walk and live a nearly independent life as a young man, had been confined to a wheelchair for most of his young life. Injured in an automobile accident when he was three, he had sustained a T-7, T-8 break (between the seventh and eighth thoracic vertebrae or roughly halfway down the upper back). This left him paralyzed from the waist down. Robert was selected by Philadelphia's Shriners Hospital to become the first youngster ever to be fitted with FES. Researchers there regarded him as an ideal candidate because he had managed to maintain a remarkable degree of muscle strength in his body despite paralysis, and because he was highly motivated to follow the training needed to make FES pay off.[7] In January 1998, Robert had electrodes implanted in nerves near all the leg muscles and a computer chip embedded in his abdomen. He was on his feet almost immediately, and two months after surgery he was able to take his first steps.

Robert will probably have to use braces and crutches for the rest of his life, but he can now get around with remarkable speed and agility. On waking each day, Robert simply puts on his radio antenna and slips the controls—an on/off switch—over his thumb. He can then stand, walk, or sit on cue. Fey says of his remarkable transformation: "In my dreams, I see myself walking. This surgery was a dream for me."[8]

The Power of Speech

Losing the ability to speak is a relatively rare occurrence. But to the 5,000 to 10,000 North Americans who are currently so afflicted each year, the imposed silence can be severely disabling. A facility we usually take for granted—ordinary social communication—becomes extremely difficult. The primary cause of voice loss is a mechanical problem, involving damage to the throat's larynx, or "voice box.

To understand what goes wrong in mechanical speech loss, and how this can be overcome by manufactured devices, it's first necessary to picture what is involved in normal voice production. When we speak, air is forced up from the lungs as in breathing; at the same time, the ligaments or vocal cords that are normally held separate draw together and vibrate. The degree of tension placed on the cords changes the pitch, like tuning strings on a guitar; relaxed cords produce lower notes and more tautly drawn cords produce higher notes. The mouth cavity, tongue, teeth, lips, nose, and sinuses act as a system of valves and filters that finally produce articulated, or shaped, sounds, including distinct words. Normal vocal abilities are lost when the vocal cords become paralyzed, weakened, or destroyed as the result of throat cancer, stroke, or some kind of physical injury. Here is where inventiveness comes into play, applying various artificial aids together with speech therapy to restore a surprising degree of voice capacity to people with these injuries.

Attempts at creating an artificial larynx date from the middle of the nineteenth century, when various reedlike devices and underarm bellows were tried as a means of pumping air and producing modulated sounds. Alexander Graham Bell, inventor of the telephone, tried his own version of this device when he was still a boy—he had become interested in speech problems by observing his father's and grandfather's work with the deaf. Young Bell claimed to produce several intelligible words with his contraption, but other projects soon distracted him and the artificial voicemaker was eventually abandoned. The cause was taken up again in 1929, when researchers at AT&T Bell Laboratories attempted to re-create speech through a crude mechanical device—a tube containing a metallic reed—inserted through an artificial opening in the speaker's throat. Still later devices added battery power and controls for pitch and loudness. While skilled users were able to shape words with the Bell Labs' devices, the sounds generally lacked human qualities and the process proved clumsy.

Approaches to producing voice artificially have come a long way since then. Today's devices fall into two broad categories. The first is extrinsic, meaning it is worn outside the body. The typical extrinsic source consists of an electronically operated vibrator that is held against the speaker's throat; its vibrations pass through the tissues of the neck where they become available as vocal tone. As in natural speech, the lungs provide needed air power, and the various parts of the mouth and nose shape the sounds to produce words. The second category of artificial voice is intrinsic, in that parts of the system are surgically implanted within the throat, or in one design, implanted in the teeth. Intrinsic sound relies on the ability of the individual to work the upper end of the digestive tube (the esophagus) to do the work once done by the vocal cords. To produce esophageal speech the speaker must swallow air, move it across the esophagus so that it creates vibration, and then expel it through the oral cavity as in normal speech. People who retrain themselves to speak in this manner generally speak in a stop-and-go pattern, necessary for keeping the air moving in sufficient volume.

A newer method of restoring speech is designed to help patients whose vocal cords are still fully or even partially intact but too weak to vibrate without some help. It consists of implants, shaped like the heads of tiny hammers and made of a chalk-like substance acceptable to the human immune system. The function of the implants is to provide sufficient bulk to make the damaged cords thicker and consequently to meet or nearly so. In this way they are able to channel and trap air effectively and thus to vibrate in the way that produces nearly normal sound. The surgery needed to accomplish this is remarkably simple. Under local anesthesia, the doctor makes a small hole in the neck, drilling through the thyroid cartilage, or Adam's apple, to reach the vocal cords behind. Temporary devices in five different sizes are inserted into the cords as the patient "tries out" the resulting voice. When the patient hears the sound that seems closest to normal, the temporary is replaced with a permanent implant of the same size. No sooner is the hole in the neck closed than the patient is able to speak, though it may take several weeks before the implant is thoroughly absorbed into the vocal cords and the patient gains full control of speech.

Nerve and brain damage, either from head injury, stroke, or a neurological disease, can also cause a form of speech loss known as aphasia. In this instance, the areas of the brain where the mental processes of language formation and the motor processes required to direct the muscles of speech originate are no longer able to function. Not only speech but the ability to read, write, and comprehend what others are saying may also be affected. This is one sensory disorder that does not yet have a high-tech solution.

5 ONE KID'S JOURNEY ON THE ROAD TO RECOVERY

For all the extraordinary progress that has been made in repairing damaged bodies, it should never be imagined that needing and receiving a replacement organ or limb are anything but traumatic. Many people to whom this has happened, and most particularly amputees, report that the first feelings of waking from surgery and finding a familiar part of the body missing or changed forever is downright terrifying. It's as though the person who was once there has died and a stranger has taken over. They commonly feel emotionally overwhelmed, helpless, grief-stricken, even lonely. Many new amputees imagine themselves no longer lovable, or think they have changed so dramatically that no one they care about will even know them any longer. These are, of course, exaggerated fears; with time, the majority of amputees master their new situation and regain confidence and a sense of "wholeness." It often takes months of work and the assistance of many skilled people, as well as the support of family and friends, to get there. In time, however, most people find that they can resume an essentially normal life.

For those who were born with congenital abnormalities, such as a missing or deformed limb, amputation surgery and rehabilitation can be the first chapter in a life that will change dramatically for the better. For the first time, perhaps, they will know the freedom to move and participate on close to equal footing with their peers.

Being an amputee is not as rare a condition as one might think. Today, almost four million Americans are amputees. Of these, three-quarters have lost one or more limbs as the result of a life-threatening disease. Among adults, the predisposing factor is most often uncontrolled diabetes or some other condition that affects blood circulation; among children, it's bone cancers. Slightly more than 20 percent of amputations are traced to accidents. Many arms, hands, fingers, and feet are severed in on-the-job accidents on farm or in factory; lawnmower, workshop, and chain-saw accidents are all too common on home turf. Bones and nerves and arteries may also be crushed beyond repair in car and sporting accidents or lost to violence in wartime, in natural disasters, or through gunshot wounds. Only a very small percentage—as little as 3 percent—of amputations are due to developmental and birth injuries resulting in limbs sufficiently deformed to require surgical removal.

The statistics on the causes of limb loss are somewhat different in other countries, owing to the kinds of hazards that people encounter in their particular environments. In countries where land mines have been an instrument of warfare, stepping on explosive devices remains a constant danger long after peace returns. According to international estimates, more than 115 million land mines lie buried on battlefields, the majority in East Asia. People in the rural areas of these countries risk injury every day as they go about their ordinary routines of farming, herding animals, and walking along country paths. In Cambodia, for example, despite the government's efforts to remove land mines buried during civil war and hostilities with bordering countries, accidental loss of limbs due to exploding land mines still occurs at a rate of more than 200 victims per month.[3] The situation is only moderately better in Vietnam, where the war ended in 1973. Worse still, mutilation—the lopping off of hands or feet—is used as a specific tool of warfare in a few countries, most recently in Sierra Leone, where rebel troops attacked civilians indiscriminately in January 1999.

painful beginnings

Let us try to put a human face on what it means to go through the experience of losing a limb. We have chosen as our example an otherwise normal American teenager whom we will call Jeremy Brown (not his real name). Though everyone's journey toward recovery is to some extent unique, Jeremy's story is fairly typical in its broad outlines. Let Jeremy give us some background:

> I have always loved sports. In fact I can't remember a time when I wasn't playing ball or riding a bicycle or running. But just before my 14th birthday I was in a serious accident. My best friend Nick and I were climbing around an old stone quarry near my house, when I lost my grip and fell about 20 feet [5 meters]. Luckily, I came to rest against a tree root, but a huge boulder rolled down on my left leg and crushed it. I passed out almost instantly, but Nick had the good sense to run for help. Pretty soon the fire department and the ambulance crew showed up and got me out of there. Next thing I knew I was lying on a table in the hospital emergency room staring up at my mom and dad. They looked really frightened.
>
> Dr. Harding, the hospital's orthopedist, came in to examine me. He told me I was "a lucky

boy" because I hadn't hit my head too hard. But he said that my lower left leg was shattered and torn up. He said he would try to put it back together, but he couldn't make any promises. He could see that the bone was in lots of pieces and the arteries were messed up. Even if he could reconstruct them, my leg could become badly infected from all the dirt and stuff that got in there, and if that happened, I might have to have the leg amputated. Then he had me rolled around to the X-ray room for some pictures. By the time the X rays were back, Dr. Liebman, the vascular surgeon, had come to see me too. He said pretty much the same thing. You can imagine that I wasn't too happy about the news! In fact, I was grossed out, and my parents weren't much better.

The doctors gave me some powerful pain injection to make me lie still and then went to work on my leg, cleaning up the wounds and setting the bones. But every now and then I could hear them muttering. It didn't sound good. After a few days in the hospital, the infection kicked in as they had predicted. None of the antibiotics they tried had more than a temporary effect. Dr. Harding told me that cutting off my leg was the only "cure" they could offer at that point. I figured I was going to be stuck doing wheelies in a chair for the rest of my life. But he said that he personally knew some terrific athletes who had overcome similar disasters and that he could get me up and walking in just a few days if I was willing to work at it.

I decided pretty quick that I didn't really have any other choice. I had to try to make the best of the situation or I was toast.

Jeremy was operated on on February 12, 1997. Fortunately, Dr. Harding and Dr. Liebman were able to save the knee, but the part below that had to be amputated. That meant that some major muscles important to walking could be kept intact and also that the prosthesis itself could be less weighty and less complicated mechanically. The operation went smoothly, and he was back in his room within a few hours. Jeremy describes what happened next:

> When I got back from the operation, I was feeling nothing. In fact, I thought I still had my leg until I lifted the sheet. When I saw what was there, I felt sick to my stomach. My left foot and the bottom part of that leg were gone. My knee was wrapped in a rigid dressing made of plaster of Paris. And the whole thing hurt, right down to the toes, which seemed pretty peculiar, considering that I didn't have any real toes. I tried not to cry, but I couldn't stop. My mom and dad were crying too. Pretty soon, Dr. Harding, the surgeon, came into the room. He told me he knew I felt scared, but that I was about to discover some new things about myself and just how adaptable the human body is when it has to be. He said that my attitude and determination were going to be very important to me in the next few weeks and that I was about to meet a "team" of people who were going to help me get back on my feet, literally. All I could think was, "Yeah, right."

Over the next few days, Jeremy was kept pretty busy. Both Dr. Harding and Dr. Liebman came around to see him every day to check on his progress, especially how he was healing. And a nurse came in to check on his residual stump. The greatest concern at this stage is edema, which is swelling caused by fluid collecting in the stump. The rigid cast is supposed to discourage that, but it has to be checked several times a day at first.

Jeremy's physical therapist, Andrea Cason (not her real name), started working with him, too. Physical therapists are professionals with advanced training in the use of bones and muscles to achieve movement. They treat a wide range of injuries and disorders using physical methods, including active and passive exercises and massage, usually in consultation with a physician or surgeon. Andrea said that artificial limbs were amazing devices, but that all the high-tech gizmos in the world wouldn't matter if Jeremy didn't work at his own rehabilitation. She also warned that he would almost certainly have days when he felt discouraged, sad, or angry, but that this was part of the natural process of rehabilitation. His whole "team" would be there to help him through tough times, but he had to be willing to talk about problems and fears when they arose.

Andrea went on to say that the first step in getting Jeremy back on his feet was to start exercising his leg even before he could stand on it, so that his remaining leg muscles did not tighten and contract. They would begin by "desensitizing" the residual limb by touch. Desensitization has a physical purpose—it reduces nerve irritation and aids blood circulation, which in turn speeds wound healing—but, just as important, it helps the patient learn to accept the amputation psychologically. Jeremy shuddered at the thought. He had not wanted to even look at his stump, much less touch or stroke or massage it, but Andrea gently insisted as she took him through all the stages. Then she had him lift the stump, move it around, and even slap it gently with the heel of

111

his hand. She told Jeremy to pay special attention to feeling the muscles in his thigh and to noticing that they were still strong and resilient. She then helped Jeremy to get up out of bed and stand, putting all his weight on his natural leg while supporting and steadying himself with crutches. She talked to him about relearning how to balance himself now that his body weight was distributed differently.

After helping him shift to his temporary transportation—a wheelchair—the two of them headed down to the rehabilitation wing of the hospital. There she introduced him to a couple of other young leg amputees who were getting set to go home the following day. Jeremy watched as 15-year-old Andy and 11-year-old Sarah each took a couple of awkward steps. He was encouraged to see that though walking slowly, they were very much moving on their own.

standing tall

The following day Jeremy's prosthetist, Bill Galiano (not his real name), came by to see how he was doing. Bill started by telling Jeremy that he knew where Jeremy was coming from. He pulled up both trouser legs to reveal that he, too, had been "retrofitted," as he liked to say.

> I got these two legs as the result of doing time in Vietnam some years ago. When I came back, I was given the best that the Veterans Administration had to offer at the time, and in the process of getting back on my feet, I discovered that I had found my job in life. I went back to school, got my college degree, and then went on to take post-college professional training. You learn about biomechanics and materials engineering and anatomy. And most especially, you get training in how to design,

make, and assemble prosthesis parts. As a matter of fact, I had a hand in making the legs I'm wearing. And now I'm going to do at least as well for you, probably better, because young guys like you usually adapt very fast.

Jeremy liked Bill immediately, and he found his upbeat manner and enthusiasm for his work reassuring. Bill said he had looked in on the unconscious Jeremy during surgery, had measured his residual leg, and had assembled for him an I-POP, which he explained, stands for Immediate Post-Operative Prosthesis. He told Jeremy not to be alarmed at the appearance of this first appliance, that it would soon be replaced with a more functional but still unfinished prosthesis, and that this in turn would be followed by a "definitive" fully customized appliance in perhaps three months, when everything had stabilized. Bill said that even with his I-POP, Jeremy could be walking and doing toe-touches in five days. For the moment, however, he should take heart in just standing still.

Andrea then got Jeremy into his harness, while Bill fixed a rig with an aluminum tubelike peg leg and "foot" to his stump and made some adjustments in the overall fit. Then they brought over a couple of ordinary bathroom scales and had Jeremy stand with his able-bodied leg on one, his I-POP on the other. They told him to shift from side to side so that one scale read 20 pounds (9 kg) and the other had most of his weight. Andrea explained that this was to make him aware of how he was distributing his weight. All Jeremy could think about, however, was how much less he weighed since giving up his left foot and lower leg.

Satisfied that they had made a good beginning, Bill looked in on another patient, while Andrea worked with Jeremy on taking a few steps using crutches. As a leg amputee, he had to overcome his natural fear of falling.

When she saw that Jeremy was pretty tired, she ended the day's exercises, helped him remove his I-POP, and checked his stump for sore places. She was glad to report that everything looked good. Nothing appeared to be taking undue pressure in the socket, the stitched area was healing nicely, and his skin was a healthy pinkish color, showing that blood circulation was normal. She told him to take a spin in his wheelchair, get a good night's sleep, and look for her tomorrow.

On Day Four, Jeremy's surgeons pronounced him far enough along to move to the rehab wing of the hospital for a few days of more intensive therapy and practice.

moving on

Before lunchtime, Jeremy was relocated to a room on the rehab floor. He found the atmosphere quite different than in the rest of the hospital. Everywhere he looked, people were dressed normally rather than wearing pajamas, and far from being in bed, they were constantly busy, almost like being in school. Some were marching up and down the corridor, others were stretching or using exercise machines, or going to and from what seemed to be a steam room or swimming pool. Though many of them moved a little unevenly, they seemed for the most part to be fully engaged in what they were doing. He noticed that music was playing in every exercise room and lots of noise and loud conversation.

He was beginning to feel less like a sick person in this lively company. Jeremy recalled:

> My leg felt pretty good, except for times when I would wake up with what they explained was "phantom pain," but I really wanted to get on home, so I worked at whatever Andrea and the others told me to do. I spent hours wearing my I-POP. I got so used to it that I named it Fred,

don't ask me why. One thing that Andrea was big on was showing me how to put my prostheses on and off, especially how to ensure that it always fits properly. The probiem is that the stump size keeps changing. Mine was getting a tiny bit smaller each day as it healed and the swelling went down. She showed me how to make the socket fit smoothly by adding layers of prosthetic sock as needed.

She also talked to me about "hygiene." Not the kind they teach you in school, but special things to do to keep the amputation area clean and dry. It gets really hot inside the plastic socket because body heat is trapped there and the leg sweats a lot more than it used to. She said it's because I lost some of my natural air-conditioning when I lost my lower leg: there's less skin surface to do the cooling. She told me that I should get used to cleaning the whole rig, stump, socket, socks and all, at least once a day.

We also talked about the phantom pain thing. She said that it's common to feel sensations—sometimes tingling, sometimes real pain—where the limb once was, and not to pay any attention to anyone who tells me that I'm crazy or just imagining it. The sensations are real. That's because the nerves in the remaining stump continue to send messages to the brain as though everything was still connected. She promised that the sensations would diminish and probably disappear altogether with time.

"Meanwhile, she showed me how to do some mental exercises, like visualizing the missing leg and foot and exercising them in my mind as I do the real exercises with my other leg and foot. I was surprised to find that the mental exercises helped some, but believe me, phantom pain is really weird. When I wasn't walking or doing balance exercises, they had me watching videos about amputees who were doing all kinds of amazing things. One guy, who had been born without feet, had become a competitive sprinter, and raced in the 100-meter at the Paralympics in Atlanta, Georgia, in 1996. He came within a couple of seconds of beating the world record—and that had been set by an able-bodied runner! Another guy the video showed was a professional singer and dancer on Broadway. And there was a kid who had made it all the way to the varsity basketball team at some Big Ten University on one good leg and one fancy one. They were basically people who came from ordinary places and were living ordinary lives, but with prostheses that you could see and relate to. Most of them talked about their experience, and how they had gradually adjusted to their changed bodies and physical abilities.

I decided that if they could do it, maybe I could too. I was willing to try whatever it took to get back to being normal. About a week after arriving there, Dr. Harding came in to give me the good word. He was releasing me from the hospital. From then on, I was going to continue treatment as an outpatient.

out and about

In the months after the accident, Jeremy had gone a long way toward reaching his goal. He moved from his I-POP to his Preliminary Prosthesis. And he gradually worked up from wearing it a few hours each day to almost every waking hour, though he remained on crutches to keep him from putting his full weight on the residual limb. He went back to school too. Several afternoons a week he met with Andrea to continue his rehab at the local outpatient center. She worked with him on gait-training, teaching him how to walk all over again.

The below-the-knee, or B-K, patient has an easier time of it than someone who has lost a portion of limb above-the-knee, because learning to use one joint—the ankle—is easier than mastering two—ankle and knee. Still, Jeremy was dismayed at how hard it was to do something he had always taken for granted before. Andrea showed him how to shift weight from side to side, and how to use his upper leg and knee to plant and lift his artificial leg and foot with maximum grace and efficiency. Gait, she told Jeremy, is not a single method and rhythm of walking; rather, every able-bodied person has his or her own distinctive walk. Part of Jeremy's task, and hers as his physical therapist, was to find a gait that is comfortable for him. She also worked with Jeremy on the treadmill to increase his aerobic capacity, so that he had the extra reserves of energy it takes to walk with a prosthesis. Jeremy's lung capacity, she said, was already a bit above average, probably because he had always been a very active youngster, but he needed to keep what he had and add some more. Jeremy, with a B-K prosthesis, needs some 10 percent more oxygen than he did before his amputation.

Once a week Andrea took him through the "Activities of Daily Living" laboratory, an indoor obstacle course at the rehab center where patients can master various challenges like getting on and off a bus, walking on rough surfaces, climbing stairs, and getting in and out of the shower on one leg. When Jeremy groused about these tasks, Andrea told him to be glad that he didn't have to go through the routines of the arm-and-hand amputee—

relearning how to use an artificial appliance in getting dressed, in handling a fork and knife, in using a variety of writing instruments, including a computer keyboard, without the dexterity and sensitivity to touch that a natural hand or arm has.

Andrea also made it her business to assess Jeremy's state of mind; if she sensed that he was still having trouble accepting the loss of his leg, or if she picked up clues that his parents were doing too much for him, she could call in one of the center's psychologists to work with Jeremy and his family. Andrea thought the signs were encouraging. Jeremy was a quick study. He had even asked Dr. Harding if he could begin to kick a soccer ball around. Dr. Harding said that as soon as Jeremy was fitted for his permanent prosthesis and adjusted to it, he would be ready for as much activity as he could tolerate—even team sports if he wanted to.

new, cool tool

Given the green light, Jeremy's parents made an appointment to go around to Bill Galiano's prosthetics workshop to discuss options and get a fitting. Bill started the discussion by defining what he and Dr. Harding meant by "permanent." He said that no prosthesis he could provide would be truly permanent. Jeremy would almost certainly outgrow and outwear whatever he got in a couple of years, and even people who have attained full stature need a replacement at least every five years because no synthetic materials have the durability of human bones and muscles and skin. (As a matter of fact, the technology of prosthetics is improving so fast that most people become impatient for a new appliance even before the old one wears out, much the way computer users are always looking to see what's coming next.) Bill told Jeremy he had a number of choices, depending on whether he put a greater value on high performance or appearance.

118

He said that Jeremy's insurance company would almost certainly supply him with a very good first prosthesis, but that he and his parents would probably have to cover costs for replacements after that.

He added that a conventional B-K socket, leg, and foot would probably cost about $10,000 each time, more like $18,000 if Jeremy got into competitive sports. An advanced myoelectric arm and hand, by contrast, can range upwards of $50,000!

Lots of his younger below-knee clients, Bill said, seem to go for the "Darth Vader" look, which he defined as a high-tech, custom-assembled version of the I-POP. It's a sleek, very durable, all black pylon or shank made of carbon steel, fiberglass, and epoxy, with all the fancy shock-absorbers and other elements visible in its open frame.

Alternatively, Bill said, he could give Jeremy a prosthesis that looked really natural on the outside. The life-like version also had a pylon inside to provide the rigidity and strength needed for walking and other movements, but there was an outside part consisting of a layer of foamy material over which was stretched a thin layer of rubberized skin. Colored to match the wearer's flesh tone, this cosmetic leg looks and feels almost natural to the touch. And it's waterproof. It can even be worn swimming, which is something not recommended for the stripped-down, lean and mean, high-performance pylon. The real disadvantage of the lifelike version is that it can't take the kind of abuse that youngsters like Jeremy would give it. Bill also discussed foot choices.

While it is still possible to buy a rubber and wood foot that is molded to look remarkably natural, down to ten perfect toe nails, he recommended going for high performance over appearance here too. He suggested a unit that combined shock-absorbing capabilities with energy-storing features similar to those in the natural arched foot. Particularly good for active amputees is a spring-loaded carbon fiber device that looks more like something you would find under the hood of a sports car than it does like a foot. Bill said that this high-tech version equips the wearer for natural ankle motion—side to side as well as front to back flexibility, important for anyone walking on uneven ground outdoors. It also gives a smooth, even stride that stiffens as the user applies more force and weight, which is important in running. And its ingenious heel design actually propels the wearer forward each time the appliance strikes the ground, action that tends to put bounce in the step and cancel the passive weight of the lower leg.

Jeremy picks up the story again. "I knew immediately which was right for me. I wanted the high-performance hardware like the athletes in Andrea's videos wore. Though I've had times when I've been depressed about losing my leg, I am not going to try and disguise my situation. I think these gizmos look pretty cool, all things considered."

the right stuff

Bill then proceeded with his final measurements. The permanent socket, which interfaces with the living stump, takes the longest to get right because it, more than any other part, must be perfect. As Bill told Jeremy, it has several jobs to do. The socket contains and protects the residual limb; it provides an anchorage for the prosthesis; and it is the site where the forces of movement and gravity are transferred from the body to the artificial limb and back again.

Each residual limb has a unique three-dimensional shape, based on the location of the surgical amputation and the person's height, weight, and muscular configuration. Bill already had a considerable amount of information based on the I-POP and the preliminary socket that

120

Jeremy had been using for the past several weeks, but he had to make one more definitive fit with a residual limb that had by now found its normal size. Of course, as Jeremy grows, the circumference of the stump may well increase, but Bill hoped that won't happen soon.

When Bill first started making sockets, he had to do virtually every step by hand, wrapping wet plaster of Paris bandages over the residual limb, letting them dry, and coming away with a stiff cast from which to make the plastic socket, a process that could take days. Now, however, he can produce a definitive socket in less than an hour. He relies on a computer-aided design (CAD) program to take the needed measurements and design the socket. Then, using the results, another computer-aided machine (CAM) creates a positive plaster model of the residual limb in 10 to 15 minutes. Finally, Bill uses another machine to inject plastic into the mold that produces the finished plastic socket. The other components of Jeremy's prosthesis are "off-the-shelf" items, which he had to order from one or more of several dozen U.S. component manufacturers. Bill promised to call Jeremy when he had them assembled and ready for a tryout.

A week later Jeremy was back in Bill's workshop, and as promised, everything was ready, or nearly so. Bill helped Jeremy into the socket and showed him how to adjust the pressure-fit sleeve that would hold his B-K in place. He had Jeremy stand, then walk, after which he individualized the prosthesis ever so subtly to achieve "dynamic alignment," by adjusting the various parts so that the body's weight is transferred smoothly through the stump to the foot. Within an hour, Bill pronounced Jeremy "ready to roll" and Jeremy, moving cautiously at first, took a turn or two around the room and said it felt "pretty good."

Jeremy has been back to see Bill several times since that big day for regular checkups and adjustments.

Things are going remarkably well, considering how dark the outlook seemed six months before. He's actually running now, not as fast as he did before the accident, but improving steadily, and he thinks it's possible that he will catch up to his old self eventually. Jeremy has read predictions that bionic athletes may someday outrun and outjump able-bodied athletes, given the way bio-engineers are pushing things. He's pretty good about doing his aerobic work too, even though he has to do it on his own now that his prescription for rehabilitation has run its course. And he walks fairly normally, so that his friends at school often forget that he has an artificial leg and foot except when something untoward happens.

He laughed as he told Bill about a soccer scrimmage he was in. "Here I was, heading for an open goal, all set to be a hero. I went to kick the ball real hard, all of a sudden I felt 'Fred' starting to let go. Next thing I knew, the whole thing—socket, leg, foot, and shoe—was up in the air and flying and the rest of me was heading for the dirt. 'Fred' came down just behind the goalpost, still in one piece. My friends were so busy laughing that I managed from where I was lying to give the ball a shove with my other foot. The ball went through the goal. You should have seen the look on the faces of the people watching!" Bill laughed too. "Jeremy, you're learning fast. Good equip-ment and a strong will are important to an amputee for sure, but nothing is more valuable in this business than having a sense of humor."

6 BRAVE NEW WORLDS

In repairing injured and broken bodies, we have certainly come a long way from the peg legs and splints that our ancient forebears had to rely on. However, if you know someone who has a seriously damaged heart or kidney or liver, or a child born with a serious birth defect, you also know that in some areas medicine is still frustrated in its search for reliable remedies.

One of the most troubling areas is in transplantation or organs. Doctors are able to save tens of thousands of lives each year through transplantation, but they do not begin to have sufficient donor organs to take care of all those in desperate need. In 1993, for example, roughly 138,000 Americans were awaiting a new heart, lung, liver, kidney, or pancreas. Sadly, fewer than one-quarter of these people ultimately got them. The other three-quarters either died an early death or continued to live in a restricted manner, many of them bound to a life-sustaining machine. For some of them, a compatible donor organ could not be found in time. But for fully half—perhaps as many as 70,000—their names never even made it onto one of the highly selective waiting lists. The committees of doctors, social workers, psychologists, and hospital administrators who are entrusted to make such life-and-death decisions judged that these individuals simply did not meet the restrictive criteria by which recipients for precious body repair parts are chosen. And as the demand for organs continues to grow, the already huge shortfall in the supply of human organs will probably increase and the task of the committees grow more complex.

a gift beyond measure

This inability to make a lifesaving procedure available to all who need it could be greatly relieved if more people knew about and were willing to choose organ donation as an option in the unlikely instance that they die someday as the result of an accident. (As many as 15,000 potential donors die of brain death in the United States each year, but in only a third of such cases is the decision made to donate.) Would-be donors need only make their desires known to relatives in advance and carry a legal donor card. The offer is then exercised only if the donor's injury is judged fatal and surgical "harvest" of their undamaged organs can be completed in a timely fashion. (Surgical removal must be done in a hospital in that brief period between brain death and the moment when the heart ceases to beat.) A person is legally and medically dead, and thus a suitable candidate for donating organs, when physicians examining the body declare that the brain has stopped functioning. The heart and other vital organs are then kept alive by a mechanical ventilator while members of the transplant network speedily arrange a match with a patient in need.

There are two notable exceptions to the brain-dead requirement for organ procurement: kidneys and bone marrow. These organs can be donated by healthy, living donors according to a more deliberate timetable. In the

124

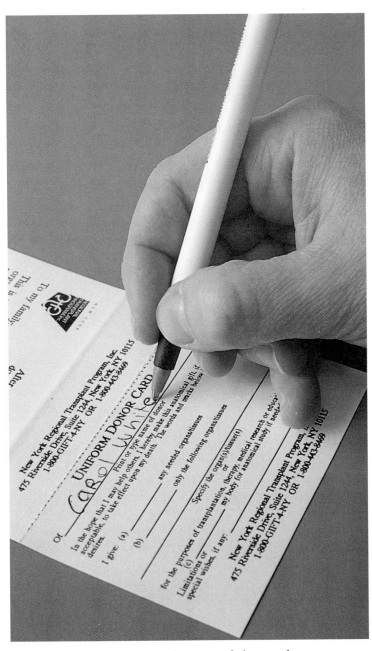

A wallet-sized organ donor card, honored in every U.S. state without obstruction or delays.

case of kidneys, you will remember from the description in Chapter 3 that humans are typically born with a "spare" kidney that can be given to another needy individual without undue harm to the donor. Similarly, bone marrow is a precious substance that our bodies produce and replenish at a constant rate, so it too can be donated to save another's life without endangering the donor's health.

Almost anyone—from infancy to age 65 or even older—can become a potential donor. The essential requirement is that the donor be in basic good health, with no history of chronic disease, infection, or cancers. Even when an individual's heart stops before organ donation can be arranged, tissues such as bone, skin, ligaments, tendons, muscles, heart valves, and corneas may still be donated.

Also, in many instances, a single donor is able to help many fortunate recipients. When in 1994, for example, a seven-year-old California boy named Nicholas Green was fatally shot by bandits while on holiday with his family in Italy, his body was rushed to a nearby hospital. Devastated as his parents were by the loss of their child, they decided immediately to offer Nicholas's healthy organs to others in need. As a result, seven people, most of them Italian children, were given a second chance at life. Asked some months later about the decision to donate their young son's organs, Nicholas's father said it had been the only right choice for the family. "The joy in seeing so much eager young life that would otherwise have been lost, and the relief in their families' faces, is so uplifting that it has given some sort of recompense for what otherwise would have been just a sordid act of violence."[3]

According to a government study, one of the prime reasons that so many people are reluctant to think about organ donation are the many misconceptions and myths concerning organ donation and transplantation.[4] Some people, for example, believe that the majority of donor organs used in the United States are bought and sold through illegal sources, such as the black market. The fact is that Congress made sure this would not happen by passing, in 1984, the National Organ Transplant Act, which prohibits such trade. All organ donations must be made freely and without any payment in exchange. Any person, including a family member, caught buying or selling an organ is subject to large fines and imprisonment. As the procuring and transplanting of organs require so many skilled physicians and other health professionals, working in such elaborate facilities under tremendous scrutiny, it's hard to imagine that any sort of piracy or secret negotiations could go on in the United States, fictional movie plots to the contrary.

Other people believe that dying patients in hospitals are hurried to their death just so someone else can have their heart or some other needed organ. The fact is that the rules and regulations protecting the dying are extremely rigid. "Brain death" must occur before donation is considered, and no one involved in carrying out the actual transplant is able to influence the moment at which brain death is officially declared. Hospitals are required to use different doctors—usually including a neurologist—to determine independently the status of the donor before organ harvesting can begin. Still another frequently heard rumor is that racial discrimination plays a role in organ distribution. On the contrary, the real obstacle to members of racial minorities receiving transplant organs is the same one that affects everyone else— organ compatibility. Many transplant situations require close genetic matching, and a donor and recipient from the same racial group are more likely to make an acceptable match than people of different racial groups. Unfortunately, relatively few people of color register as donors. As long as this situation persists, the opportunities for candidates of similar genetic makeup to receive compatible organ donations will be disproportionately smaller than those of candidates of Western European heritage.

Lastly, there is the widely held belief that people who receive organ transplants also receive some of the traits and attitudes of their donors. In fact, there is no scientific basis for such psychological "memories" being passed along with a transplant. No doubt that the experience of being given a second chance at life can have profound psychological effects on some recipients, and this can inspire them to adopt new behaviors, but these don't come along with the organs. If certain similarities between donor and recipient are later detected, it's probably a case of coincidence, or the result of something overheard in the hospital during the patient's recovery that influences the change. Possibly, it's the power of suggestion at work. Sometimes the recipient learns something about the donor from reading the news or talking to the donor's family and unconsciously adopts some of the donor's ways.

between brain death and new life

You may wonder how the matchups take place in the hours between brain death and donation. The actual transplant has to be carried out, in most instances, with extreme speed in order to preserve the organ's viability. Even as the brain-dead donor is being prepared for the surgery that will remove one or more donated organs, blood tests are performed. These tests establish blood type and confirm that no detectable infection or underlying disease is present in the donor that might be passed on to the recipient.

At the same time, transplant counselors complete arrangements with the donor's family, a process that can be both sad—for the loss of a loved one—and joyous—because they realize that a great good is about to happen

128

Transplant organs can live outside the body for only a few hours. A nurse hand-carries an organ donation in an ice cooler to a waiting helicopter.

to another person and another family. Meanwhile, the national organization known as the United Network for Organ Sharing (UNOS) is alerted to the imminent availability of one or more donor organs. Since 1984, UNOS has served as a central computerized clearinghouse for the many state and regional procurement organizations and transplant centers around the country.

Staffed 24 hours a day, 365 days a year, UNOS keeps information on every American who has been chosen as a qualified organ recipient by his or her regional transplant board. The UNOS staff generates an updated list of potential recipients, ranking them according to certain criteria—blood type, tissue type, size of the organ, medical urgency of the patient, time spent on the waiting list, and physical distance between the donor and recipient. The average wait is about three years. Once the prime candidate has been identified, UNOS contacts the hospital and transplant surgeon responsible for that patient to offer one or more requested organs. If for some reason the surgeon decides that the particular timing or match is not desirable—perhaps the recipient is in particularly fragile health that week—and rejects the offer, the Organ Center contacts the next candidate and surgeon on the list. Once the match is established, however, arrangements to transport the refrigerated organ, usually by special air courier, are made.

Though the requirements for different organs vary somewhat, speed is generally a high priority. Under current procedures and preservation methods, four hours is generally regarded as the optimum time in which to carry out the entire process from the brain death of donor to the surgical transplant in the recipient.

legal and ethical issues

The continuing shortage of usable donor organs presents society with a number of vexing legal and ethical issues.

On what basis should some people be chosen—and returned to productive life—and others be rejected? Until very recently, transplant committees at the various specialized transplant centers around the country have acted with almost perfect autonomy. Each committee has set the criteria by which candidates in their jurisdiction would be judged.

Many hospitals, recognizing just how difficult such decisions are, include on their transplant selection board a medical ethicist—a person with training in philosophy as well as medicine. The ethicist participates by helping the committee examine the ethical and moral bases on which to make such choices. Also, some external guidelines for making choices fairly and equitably are in place; they are imposed much as federal civil-rights laws are, through federal regulations. Even with guidelines, however, the process involved in choosing candidates for the transplant waiting list is never easy.

First, the committee must evaluate genuine need. It's not enough to have an imperfect heart, for example; the potential recipient's heart must be so diseased that medications and lifestyle changes cannot sustain its function for more than a few months or years without replacement. Then there is the patient's ability to withstand major surgery; he or she must be strong and otherwise healthy enough to have a fair chance of surviving the risky operation and going through the months of follow-up rehabilitation. The committee may also consider more subjective issues, though in doing so they may challenge many of the beliefs about fairness and equality that underlie democracy.

For example, should the committee give preference to the needs of a 16-year-old girl over that of a 60-year-old man simply because the younger person has a longer life ahead in which to benefit from such a gift? Or if recovery and rehabilitation after transplant are likely to require a lot of social supports and steady habits, should the person with the more conventional set of behavior patterns be put ahead of the person with the more free-form and venturesome lifestyle? In other words, should a person who has a loving family and a job and a record of taking his or her medications regularly receive preference over a single person with an unconventional lifestyle? What about the recipient's ability to pay for a transplant? Is there any justification to the committee's using the so-called "green screen" to give the edge to recipients who can pay the entire bill? After all, the harvesting, transplant, and rehabilitation of a human liver, for example, can cost as much as $250,000. And that's even though the liver itself is "free."

Almost no recipient can pay those kinds of costs out of pocket. The usual payer is the individual's medical insurance company. But not everyone is insured: many of the poor, the unemployed, and people whose chronic health problems have made them undesirable to insurers do not have any insurance. This puts these people, who are disproportionately represented among minorities, at a subtle disadvantage in receiving transplants. Even when the hospitals and physicians do not intend to discriminate, it is difficult for the transplant committee to accept large numbers of uninsured patients for such costly procedures for fear of bankrupting the hospital. One way that is sometimes suggested is to permit a certain percentage of candidates who are willing to pay substantially more than their share of the costs to go to the top of the list, using the surplus dollars to fund the less fortunate. Many people would argue, however, that no one should be able to buy life just because he or she is rich, no matter what other benefits might result.

A whole other category of issues concern the "rights" of people whose behaviors or actions have actively and substantially contributed to their need for a transplant.

Take, for example, the person whose alcoholism has caused him or her to destroy their liver, or the person who, in a failed suicide attempt, has overdosed on some drug that has caused liver failure. Do they deserve to be treated on a par with ordinary citizens whose need for a transplant is the result of a chance illness or an accident? When Mickey Mantle, a legendary slugger for the New York Yankees, was given a liver transplant in 1995, many people cried "foul ball" because Mantle's diseased liver had been destroyed by his equally legendary drinking habits. And what about people who have criminal records? Or people who are mentally challenged? Or people who are not citizens of the same country as the donor? Should transplant committees use these factors in making their selections, or must they ignore them? Clearly, there are no easy answers, but in an effort to bring some order to the selection process, in 1999 the Department of Health and Human Services stepped in to study the disparities and to issue new guidelines. Their final report has not, as yet, been issued.

of pigs and pokes

Two highly controversial solutions to the organ shortages are currently available. One is the practice of buying organs from Third World countries. The other is something known as xenotransplantation or cross-transplantation. Let's look at each idea in greater detail. Despite the widespread poverty that exists in many Third World countries, the number of transplant operations that are conducted in some of them is remarkably high. This is because some countries have a policy that permits the outright sale of organs to foreigners willing to pay for them.

One country where this occurs is China, whose hospitals do as much as 15 percent of their transplant "business" on foreign nationals, many of them people of

Chinese ancestry who live in other parts of the world but come to China for lifesaving surgery. For China's money-starved economy, the opportunity to conduct high-priced transplants is a welcome source of foreign currency. China's policies are additionally criticized because of the way organ donations are secured. While the general practice of selling organs is condemned in most Western countries, China as a totalitarian Communist nation recognizes no such constraints.

According to reports made by international human-rights organizations, many of China's organ donations are anything but voluntary. Indeed, the organs are said to be taken from executed Chinese political prisoners, whose executions may in fact be timed to match the surgical schedules of hospitals. The practice of selling organs has become so bold, in fact, that organ "brokers" have actually been caught soliciting recipients in other countries; two agents carrying price lists for various organs were arrested by the FBI in New York in 1998. Clearly, this practice is in violation of medical and human-rights ethics and has been roundly condemned by the U.S. government as well as the international medical community.

Another option, xenotransplantation, describes the human use of organs and tissues taken from other animal species. The word derives from the Greek *xenos*, meaning strange or foreign. Improbable as using other species as a source of human spare parts may sound, it has been shown to work surprisingly well. So far, most experience has been gained in temporary "bridge" organs, implanted while recipients wait for the right human versions to come along. Another category of xenotransplant still in the experimental stage involves genetically altering animal organs so as to provide some unique benefit not possible in the human organ.

Since the early 1900s, multiple attempts have been made to transplant an organ from an animal into a human being. The most publicized instance was probably the xenotransplant that occurred in 1984 when "Baby Fae," a human infant with a severely disabled heart, was given a baboon heart. (The heart had been taken from a baboon primarily because the size is close to that of an infant.) With a tremendous amount of medical support, Baby Fae survived the initial surgery but lived on for only 20 days. Baboon liver transplants were also tried in the early 1990s, in instances where the recipients had had their own livers destroyed due to hepatitis B infections. The xenotransplants were thought to be preferable to human livers because baboons are resistant to the hepatitis B viruses that were still lurking in the recipients' systems. Once again, the patients died within a few weeks of surgery. But as the deaths were not related to liver failure, the practicality of the xenotransplants was never proved or disproved.

Later research has turned to xenotransplantation using pig donations. Pigs are a logical choice, not because they are similar to humans genetically—they aren't—but because they are in large supply, their organs are physically similar in size to those of humans, and they can be raised in captivity in carefully controlled, closed herds whose ancestral lineage and health status are well-documented. The idea of using animal parts to keep humans alive has always excited controversy. Animal-rights activists, who oppose using animals for any kind of experimentation, certainly regard raising animals to harvest their organs as exploitative. Also, people of some religious faiths find the idea of interfering with Nature to be contrary to their beliefs. In addition, there are some purely medical concerns. For one, the significant genetic differences between animals and humans require that any recipient of an animal organ take massive amounts of immunosuppressant drugs indefinitely to prevent rejection, a costly and potentially dangerous practice.

A still larger issue remains. Many medical authorities believe that even if the surgery is made safer and the follow-up care easier for the human recipients, we may still be opening a "Pandora's box" of long-term risks both to the health of the individuals who undergo the operations and the health of the human species as a whole. This is because the very process of exchanging genetic materials between species has the potential to introduce as yet unrecognized animal diseases into the human gene pool. Once there, these transferred diseases could mutate slightly and become lethal, passing from generation to generation of humans with devastating effects. Notorious examples of infectious agents, not transmitted through outright transplants but through living in close proximity to the animals they normally inhabit, are believed to be the viruses responsible for "swine flu" and for AIDS. Another example is "mad cow disease," a deadly form of bovine encephalitis that a number of Britons are believed to have contracted from eating diseased beef cattle, which had been raised on commercial feed containing bits of diseased sheep carcasses.

To allay fears, and at the same time continue to learn more about the suitability of animal organs in human transplantation, the U.S. Food and Drug Administration entered the arena in 1994. Working with public and private research agencies, it began to draft a lengthy set of rules and regulations regarding xenotransplant experiments. The groups are still conferring and, for the time being at least, most forms of xenotransplantation are on hold. One notable exception are human heart-valve replacements harvested from pig hearts.

designer genes

Many scientists are hailing the twenty-first century as the Biotechnology Century. That's because rapid scientific advances in biochemistry, cell biology, and the science of genetics are preparing the way for a vast new array of medicine-like substances that someday will be used to correct or repair many conditions that cause human organs to malfunction. Already benefiting from this revolution are people with diabetes and hemophilia, and children who produce insufficient amounts of growth hormone to grow to normal adult size.

The biotech breakthrough came to diabetes first. Since 1922, persons with diabetes, a pancreatic disorder that is a major cause of disability and death, have been able to control many of their symptoms by taking daily injections of insulin derived from the pancreatic glands of pigs and oxen. While these animal products were not entirely satisfactory, they did give diabetics a new chance at life. Then, in 1982, genetic scientists at Genentech and Eli Lilly, two American companies involved in advanced drug research, used a process known as recombinant DNA technology ("gene splicing") to produce human insulin in the laboratory. In simplest terms, the researchers identified the genetic building blocks, or code, for human insulin and inserted or recombined these genes in the genetic code of a common intestinal bacterium known as *Escherichia coli*. They then cultured the "improved" bacteria in vitro (in a test tube) under conditions that prompted each one of the bacteria to divide over and over again to form a mighty army of identical offspring, all of them microscopic-size insulin-producing factories. With further steps to purify and package the insulin, the hormone was ready for market in 1983 as the first of several recombinant DNA substances that would ultimately be approved for human use.

In 1985 genetically engineered human growth factor received formal FDA approval for medical use in treating children who fail to attain normal stature as the result of pituitary gland disorder. Previously, the only source of growth hormone to treat such youngsters was that har-

*A researcher records a new piece of code for
the Human Genome Project.*

vested from human corpses, a risky and expensive choice available to only a tiny fraction of those in need. And, in 1992, *E. coli* bacteria were reengineered to produce Factor VIII, an essential component in promoting blood coagulation. Prior to the development of recombinant DNA clotting factor, persons suffering from the most common forms of hemophilia, an inherited bleeding disorder, had to rely on blood-clotting concentrates taken from thousands of blood donors, another expensive and risky procedure.

Though the sequencing of human clotting factor had much in common with that of insulin and growth factor, many years elapsed between them. However, the ability of scientists to decode the entire DNA, or genome, of humans has taken a dramatic new turn. It is predicted that through a highly organized multibillion-dollar program known as the Human Genome Project, the genetic codes of each of the more than 80,000 genes in the body will be known by the end of 2003. When that time comes, scientists will be on the threshold of correcting hundreds of other diseases through processes not so different from those involved in producing human insulin through artificial means.

The presumption is that genetic diseases divide roughly into those where some bit of genetic code is missing an essential part, those genes carrying an extraneous part, and those genes with all the right parts, only arrayed in incorrect order. Gene therapy would then focus on making the necessary corrections by the appropriate insertions and/or deletions, much like restringing beads. For such single-gene error diseases as cystic fibrosis, which affects more than 30,000 Americans, the ability to make the corrective splice may not be far away. Other diseases, such as autism, involve multiple genetic anomalies, and will presumably take many years before genetic interventions are possible.

Approaching human health problems at the genetic level is dealing with human life at its most basic and most minute form. Another approach is to make repairs and replacements of damaged body parts "piecemeal" through "tissue engineering." *Tissue* is the term used to describe groups of similar cells that perform a similar function. Organs are also made up of tissues, often in layers constructed of two or more kinds, as is the case in skin, the most abundant, most visible of organs.

Tissue engineering is a new and rapidly expanding area of experimental medicine in which scientists work to develop ways to grow human tissues in the laboratory. Many medical scientists confidently predict that their research will progress to the point that doctors will be able to order up living, lab-grown livers, pancreases, ears, fingers, bones, and even hearts, whenever existing ones fail. Or better yet, they will have the tools to tinker with the body's own systems to regenerate such tissues on site.

Here in simplified terms is how tissue engineering works. The tissue engineer starts with two essential elements: a biodegradable "scaffold" and a "soup" of specialized cells. The scaffold, which is somewhat analogous to a honeycomb, only microscopic in size, is woven of either natural or synthetic materials. It can be given the shape of the tissue it is to replace—flat if it is to become skin, tubular if it is to be an artery or vein, valvelike if it is to replace a heart valve, and so on. The cellular soup is typically made up of the particular kinds of cells that would normally inhabit the tissue under construction. An alternative under investigation is the use of bone marrow cells, found in the hollow centers of bones, for the cellular soup, because under the right circumstances they can be coaxed to "morph" into whatever specialized cells are needed.

A researcher examines sheets of collagen grown in the lab.

The original models for the cells used in tissue engineering come from a human donor, perhaps even the very human who is in need of the replacement tissue. The cells are seeded on the scaffold and supplied with growth-promoting nutrients and oxygen. The whole package is then placed in the protective environment of a special incubator and left for several weeks while the cells grow and multiply and become "organized," much as they would in the human body. When they reach satisfactory density on the scaffold, the engineered tissue is ready for transplant. Once in their intended location, the transplanted cells are "smart" enough to recreate their proper tissue function. One researcher describes the process thus: "Once the cells are back in place, they say in effect 'I recognize the neighborhood and now I'm going to build a new house like the one I used to live in.'"[8]

Likewise, blood vessels attach themselves to the new tissue to supply its conventional needs for oxygen and nutrients. Finally, the biodegradable scaffold melts away leaving the tissue implant virtually indistinguishable from normal home-grown tissue.

The first practical use of this new technology is in the manufacture of artificial skin. One principal function of the skin is to protect the body against invasion by bacteria, viruses, and other foreign organisms that could cause fatal infections. About 100,000 Americans are hospitalized for serious burns every year.[9] Of these, perhaps 13,000 need skin grafts to cover areas too badly damaged to replace skin naturally.[10] Another large group needing skin grafts are people suffering from venous ulcers, usually on the legs, as the result of advanced diabetes or circulatory disorders. To repair such damage, it has long been possible to take some small natural skin grafts from elsewhere on the patient's own body—remember the nose grafts taken from arm and forehead in earlier times? However, borrowing skin in this manner has its limits; it's a little like "robbing Peter to pay Paul."

Grafts may also be taken from cadavers—dead bodies donated to science—but cadaver grafts generally work as temporary fixes at best because the recipient's body will eventually reject the donated tissue.

Work on growing artificial skin began in the mid-1970s at several medical research laboratories in the United States, but it was not until the 1990s that practical results were achieved. The living skin cells were procured from infant foreskins, the discarded by-products of ordinary hospital circumcisions. Today, this procedure has become so efficient that one Massachusetts biotech company—Organogenesis—claims to be able to produce 4 acres (1.6 hectares) of in-vitro manufactured skin from cells harvested in a single foreskin.

Following close behind in its practical application is artificial cartilage, which is being used to replace the damaged cushioning material that keeps joints flexing smoothly. At Genzyme, a leading research company working in this area, bioengineers have found a way to take a tiny sampling of the patient's own cartilage cells, multiply them rapidly in the laboratory, and reinject them in injured knees and other joints so as to achieve natural, or autologous, replacement. Considering that some 200,000 knee joints require surgical replacement each year in the United States because of cartilage deterioration, and that up to now the surgery has achieved relief but not genuine repair of the damaged knee pad, this is indeed good news.

As scientists learn more about tissue engineering, they hope to be able to make many other parts, from replacement heart valves to replacement breasts and segments of spinal cord. Perhaps the most ambitious is an international initiative launched in 1998 to grow a human heart. Its director, biomaterials professor Michael Sefton of the University of Toronto, is confident that his team will get there.

neural prostheses

In 1968, English scientists G. S. Brindley and W. Lewin were searching for a means to enrich the visual experience of the blind. They found that when an electrode was implanted in the sight region of the brain, subjects reported seeing light. This finding provoked researchers at the National Institutes of Health in the United States to begin long-term studies in what are now termed "neural prostheses."

Neural prostheses today take many forms, but basically they are brain implants of microscopic size, capable of delivering deep-brain stimulation to areas where repair or correction is needed. One such device, approved in 1997 by the FDA, helps people with Parkinson's disease to control disabling tremors by sending a constant stream of tiny electrical pulses to the specific area where the tremors arise. The same principles are being studied to control some symptoms of epilepsy, as well as Alzheimer's and Lou Gehrig's diseases, and to aid people with profound deafness whose auditory nerves are intact. Also, researchers at the Xerox Corporation are working on a device they call "Forget-Me-Not" that may someday assist people with memory lapses. Meanwhile, work continues on developing a neural prosthesis to help the blind experience truly useful artificial sight.

Progress in all these areas will not come without controversy. As has been observed in many other areas of medicine, when scientists begin to compete so boldly with Mother Nature, many groups in society have concerns. So, along with scientific progress and more dramatic discoveries to shake our concepts of what is possible, governmental, legal, and ethical authorities can be expected to weigh in too.

Body Beautiful

The skin provides the body with its principle form of protection—helping to maintain a comfortable temperature while keeping many injurious agents out and holding other key organs and systems inside, out of harm's way. Whenever skin is injured or breached in any fashion, something must be done to restore the covering. When the work is complex or extensive, it is usually a plastic surgeon who makes the repairs or corrections, which can range from stitching skin together to reconstructing both the skin and the tissue beneath that give it shape. (Incidentally, the term "plastic surgery" refers to the soft, flexible nature of skin and not to some artificial substance produced in a plastic factory.)

The earliest form of plastic surgery and reconstructive surgery is thought to have been rhinoplasty, or nose reconstruction. Though wounds, accidental mutilations, dis-ease, and birth defects such as cleft palate have created opportunities for plastic surgery as much as other forms of radical surgery, little was done in a systematic way for many centuries. Deformities, it was often remarked, were God's business, and to tamper with them was to go against His will. This attitude, of course, has changed entirely. Beginning with World War I, which inflicted many particularly disfiguring injuries on soldiers and civilians alike, it was well recognized that serious disfigurement could prevent persons affected from living happy, productive lives. Anything that could be done to reduce the disfigurement was deemed good for the individual and for society. Plastic surgery thus began to evolve into a separate medical specialty, involving both aesthetic and reconstructive procedures. (Aesthetic surgery is often defined as nonessential surgery, intended to improve a patient's self-image or correct a feature that the individual finds objectionable. Reconstructive surgery involves restoring essential function as well as more normal appearance to a damaged part of the body.) Most early plastic surgery was reconstructive, and plastic surgeons honed their skills learning to do skin grafts, which are often required in injuries caused by severe burns.

Important advances in skin-grafting techniques came with the invention of the "dermatome," a motor-driven, razor-sharp device that made it possible to cut perfectly even slices of skin in any thickness from one place on the body and use them to patch another exposed area. A later improvement led the way to "mesh grafts," by which a spiked roller was passed over the slices of lifted skin and the pieces stretched into an open weave mesh; the process thus expanded the coverage possible with each piece.

Aesthetic or cosmetic surgery is a more recent development. It includes several procedures affecting facial appearance: rhinoplasty (to reduce the size or alter the shape of the nose); otoplasty (to correct prominent ears); blepharoplasty (to remove drooping skin around the eyes); rhytidectomy (to tighten and lift skin around the entire face); chemical face peels and dermabrasion (to remove wrinkles, minor blemishes, and scars); and reconstructions and lifts of the chin and neck (for greater definition and smoothness). Also considered aesthetic surgery are two common body procedures: lipectomy (the removal of fat tissue on abdomen, thighs, and arms by suction) and breast augmentation or diminution (to alter the size of breasts). Breasts are also reconstructed following radical breast surgery, a frequent treatment for breast cancer. In the 1960s a popular method of replacing lost breast tissue was to insert a silicone-filled implant between a woman's chest wall and skin, but subsequent concerns about the possible adverse effects of silicone caused this practice to be dropped in 1992.

Today, a more common approach is to use either saline-filled implants or to rebuild the breast using the patient's own muscle, fat, and skin to do the reconstruction. Many plastic surgeons urge their patients to get psychological counseling before undertaking some forms of plastic surgery, for dissatisfaction with one's appearance may have little or nothing to do with how one actually looks. Such patients are bound to remain unhappy even after successful surgery, if the problems underlying their dissatisfaction are not addressed as well. Remarkable advances have been made in cosmetic and reconstructive plastic surgery. Some of these are in the retrieval and reuse of cartilage and bone to reconstruct deformed structures under the skin (ear lobes from rib cartilage, for example, and bone from a hip to reconstruct the lower jaw). Another exciting development is growing artificial skin, which is particularly important in providing temporary coverings for persons recovering from severe and extensive burns over the body.

SOURCE NOTES

INTRODUCTION

1. William A. Herman et al., "Future Trends in Medical Device Technology," Food and Drug Administration, Conference Report, April 8, 1998.

CHAPTER 1

1. Herodotus, *History*, Book IX, Harmondsworth, England: The Penguin Classics, 1954, pp. 566–567.
2. *Atlas of Limb Prosthetics*, American Academy of Orthopedic Surgeons, St. Louis: C.V. Mosby Co., 1981, Chapter 1 by A. Bennett Wilson Jr., p. 3.
3. Lawrence W. Friedmann, M.D., *Psychological Rehabilitation of the Amputee*, Springfield, MA: Charles Thomas, 1978, p. 11.
4. Sharon Romm, "Arms by Design: From Antiquity to the Renaissance," *Plastic and Reconstructive Surgery*, July 1988.
5. Patricia A. Padula et al., "Acquired Amputation and Prostheses Before the Sixteenth Century," *Angiology—The Journal of Vascular Diseases*, February 1987, pp. 134 ff.
6. Friedmann, p. 5.
7. Padula, idem.
8. Friedmann, p. 11.
9. Gloria T. Sanders, *Lower Limb Amputation: A Guide to Rehabilitation*, Philadelphia: F.A. Davis Co., 1986, p. 98–99.
10. idem
11. O. Fliegel, M.D., "Historical Development of Lower-Extremity Prostheses," *Archives of Physical Medicine & Rehabilitation*, May 1966, p. 277.
12. Ibid, p. 4
13. J.F. Orr et al., "The History and Development of Artificial Limbs," *Engineering in Medicine*, 1982, Vol. 11, #4, p. 156.
14. Ira M. Rutkow, M.D., *Surgery: An Illustrated History*, St. Louis: Mosby-Year Book Inc., 1993, pp. 66–67.
15. Ibid, p. 66.
16. Ibid, p. 68.
17. Ibid, p. 69.

18. Ibid, pp. 158–159.
19. Knut Haeger, *The Illustrated History of Surgery*, New York: Bell Publishing Co., 1988, p. 113.
20. Ibid, p. 112.
21. Rutkow, p. 159.
22. Ibid, pp. 168–169.
23. Ibid, p. 169.
24. Wiley F. Barker, M.D., *Clio: The Arteries, The Development of Ideas in Arterial Surgery*, Austin: R. G. Landes Co., 1992, p. 3.
25. Fielding H. Garrison, *An Introduction to the History of Medicine*, 4th edition, Philadelphia: W.B. Saunders Co., 1929, p. 225.
26. Haeger, pp. 110–111.
27. Guy Williams, *The Age of Agony, The Art of Healing 1700–1800*, Chicago: Academy Publishers, 1986, p. 181 ff.
28. Rutkow, p. 202.
29. Albert S. Lyons, M.D., and R. J. Petrucelli II, M.D., *Medicine: An Illustrated History*, New York: Abradale Press & Harry N. Abrams, 1987, p. 599.
30. Haeger, p. 145.
31. Garrison, p. 493.
32. idem, p. 488.
33. Rutkow, p. 411.
34. Audrey Davis, *Triumph over Disability: The Development of Rehabilitation Medicine in the USA*, Smithsonian Museum, Division of Medical Sciences, National Museum of History and Technology, Smithsonian, 1973, p. 32.
35. Davis, p. 32.
36. http://pele.repoc.nwu.edu/nupoc/prosHistory.html, p. 6.
37. John Duffy, *The Healers: A History of American Medicine*, Urbana, IL: University of Chicago Press, 1976, p. 127, quoting "Gunn's Manual."

CHAPTER 2
1. University of Toledo Libraries, "Medicine in the Civil War" http://www.cl.utoledo.edu/canaday/quackery/quack2.html
2. Murphy, Wendy, *Biography of William Bradley Coley*, Cancer Research Institute, privately published, 1995.
3. Ray Porter, *The Greatest Benefit to Mankind*, New York: W.W. Norton, 1997, pp. 368–369.
4. Lyons and Petrucelli II, *Medicine: An Illustrated History*, p. 503.
5. Duffy, *The Healers*, p. 220.
6. Ibid, p. 221.
7. Bell Irvin Wiley, *The Life of Billy Yank*, Baton Rouge: Louisiana State University Press, 1952, p. 148.
8. idem.

9. Stewart Brooks, *Civil War Medicine*, Springfield, IL: C.C. Thomas, 1966, p. 101
10. Sanders, p. 22.
11. Wilson D. Bennett, *History of Limb Prosthetics*, New York: Demos Publications, 6th edit., 1989, p. 6.
12. Davis, *Triumph Over Disability*, p. 37.
13. Edward T. Devine, & The Carnegie Endowment for International Peace, *Disabled Soldiers and Sailors Pensions and Training*, New York: Oxford University Press, 1919, p. 394.
14. Rutkow, *Surgery*, p. 336.
15. Ibid, pp. 344–345.
16. *Images of America*, Smithsonian Institution, Smithsonian Books, 1989, p. 34,
17. *Atlas of Limb Prosthetics*, American Academy of Orthopedic Surgeons, Chapter 1 by A. Bennett Wilson Jr., p. 3.
18. Sanders, *Lower Limb Amputation*, p. 24.
19. Davis, p. 36.
20. Wendy B. Murphy, *Healing the Generations*, Old Lyme, CT: American Physical Therapy Association and The Greenwich Publishing Group, Inc., 1995, p. 39.
21. idem.
22. Ibid, p. 68–69.
23. Devine, p. 396.
24. Ibid, p. 398.

CHAPTER 3
1. http://www.neoucom.edu/library/Chronology.html   "From Vesalius to the Pill: Selected Landmark Events in Medicine" Year 1905.
2. Porter, *The Greatest Benefit to Mankind*, p. 623.
3. Ibid, p. 610.
4. "Charles Lindbergh's Artificial Heart" by Christopher Hallowell, *American Heritage of Invention and Technology*, Fall 1985, pp. 58–62.
5. Ibid, p. 62.
6. Wendy Murphy, *The Healing Heart*, Greenwich, CT: Clinical Communications, 1998, p. 159.
7. *The New York Times*, Lillehei obituary, July 8, 1999, p. B9. "The Story of Medtronic," Medtronic, Inc., 1995; *Triumph Over Disability, The Development of Rehabilitation Medicine in the U.S.A*, Smithsonian Museum, Division of Medical Sciences, Exhibition Booklet, 1973, p. 24.
8. *FDA Consumer*, April 1994, p. 13.

CHAPTER 4

1. Margaret Rowbottom, and Charles Susskind, *Electricity and Medicine, History of their Interaction*, San Francisco Press, 1984, p. 7.
2. John Sabolich CPO, NovaCare, quoted from NovaCare "Patient Information" booklet.
3. Melvin Berger, *Bionics*, New York: Franklin Watts, 1978, p. 19.
4. *The New York Times*, Sept 21, 1999, p. F7.
5. idem,
6. On-line press release from Purdue University News Service, November 13, 1998.
7. http://www.shrinershq.org/WhatsNew/walkingtall8-98.html p. 1.
8. Ibid, p. 2.

CHAPTER 5

1. *FDA Consumer*, March 1997, p. 7.
2. Mississippi State University, "TNT Detection Goal of Mississippi State Research", press release issued October 30, 1998, quoting John Plodinec, Director of Diagnostic and Instrumentation Laboratory and statistics gathered in part from UNICEF's 1996 Report.
3. *The New York Times*, "In Cambodia, the Dying Continues Long After the War," by Seth Mydans, December 12, 1997, on-line search, p. 1,
4. *The New York Times*, "A Glimpse of the Future in the Pain of Today," October 24, 1999, Sunday Week in Review, p. 5

CHAPTER 6

1. *The New York Times*, April 5, 1998, Sunday Week In Review, p. 4.
2. www.mayohealth.org/mayo/9604/htm/organ-do.htm, Page 2.
3. www.asf.org/green.html, (The Nicholas Green Foundation) p. 4.
4. www.organdonor.gov/myth.html, pp. 1–4.
5. *The New York Times*, October 19,1999, p. 68.
6. *The New York Times*, "Arrests Put Focus on Organ Trafficking From China," by Erik Eckholm, online, February 25, 1998.
7. *The New York Times*, Sunday Week in Review, February 22, 1998, by Christopher Drew, online.
8. "The Body Builders," *Popular Science Magazine*, May 1996, p. 60.
9. *Business Week*, May 18, 1998, p. 118.
10. idem.
11. "The Body Builders," *Popular Science Magazine*, May 1996, p. 60.

GLOSSARY

amputation: the loss or removal of a body part, especially by surgical means

antigen: any substance that, when introduced in the body, stimulates the production of an antibody and often leads to rejection.

artificial limb: a manufactured device designed to replace a missing arm or leg. The replacement part may be purely "cosmetic," meaning that it is designed to look like the limb it replaces but is otherwise nonfunctioning; or it may be "functional" in that it is capable of performing one or more activities normally associated with the missing part but look distinctly different. Some of the newest artificial limbs combine both attributes.

biocompatible: relating to blood, tissues, joints, or organs—natural or artificial—that cause no reaction or rejection when transplanted or inserted in the body.

biomechanics: the science concerned with the action of forces, internal or external, on the living body, as in the study of movements involved in walking, running, and jumping, or in the activity of the heart muscle in pumping blood.

biomedical engineering: the application of various advanced engineering technologies to the field of medicine. It plays a major role in the design of modern prostheses.

bionics: a branch of biomedical engineering that emphasizes the application of biological principles to the study and design of electronic systems. The terms "bionic man" and "bionic woman" are used popularly to refer to supernatural beings who are part human, part computerized organisms.

CAD/CAM: an acronym denoting the use of computer-assisted design to produce two-dimensional images of a device; followed by computer-assisted 3-D modeling and manufacture. This relatively recent technology, which has been adopted in many areas of industrial production, has coincidentally revolutionized the manufacture of custom-made prostheses.

defibrillator: a machine designed to shock the heart's ventricular muscle and thereby restore normal beat. External units, used by emergency medical services and hospitals, include "paddles" that deliver powerful jolts through the chests of patients in cardiac arrest. Newer miniaturized units can also be implanted in the chests of at-risk patients so as to continuously monitor and intervene in heart incidents before they develop.

FES: an abbreviation for Functional Electrical Stimulation, an advanced technology that combines the data storage-and-control capacities of a computer chip with electrical implants located at key nerve sites along paralyzed muscles. With FES, the wearer with spinal cord injury is able to achieve a walking gait or movement.

gene therapy: treatment that involves the deleting or replacing of faulty genes to treat a specific genetic disorder, such as cystic fibrosis. Gene therapy exists primarily as theory, but it is expected to become a significant technique within the toolbox of medical interventions and repairs.

immune system: the body's unique and many-faceted system to protect it against the usual assaults of disease, infection, and other foreign invasions. While essential to normal survival, immunity is also a major obstacle to organ transplantation, requiring the use of immunosuppressor drugs to prevent the body from attacking its transplanted organ.

joint replacement: the surgical insertion of a knee, hip, elbow or other unit involved in the articulation of limbs. Joint replacements are typically made of highly durable and inert materials, such as stainless steel, certain plastics, and ceramics. Joint replacement is one of the most common therapies practiced today, particularly among persons suffering from arthritis or injuries from excessive use, as in sports.

myoelectric: relating to the electrical properties of muscle, and often more specifically to artificial methods of stimulating movement where normal nerve communication with muscles no longer occurs.

organ donation: the act of giving a body organ (heart, liver, kidney, lungs, pancreas, cornea) to another person. Except in the instance of a kidney donation, which can be transplanted from a living donor without adverse effect, donations are carried out immediately upon the brain death of an individual, when one or more healthy organs can be surgically removed and transplanted in a matter of hours to a compatible recipient. The decision to donate may be made in advance by a living individual, much as one writes a will, or by family members as death approaches.

orthosis, (pl. *orthoses*): an external orthopedic appliance, such as a brace or splint, that assists in the movement of the spine or limbs, particularly where normal strength and control are diminished or lacking altogether.

physical therapy: an adjunct of medical treatment that employs physical agents or forces to retrain and/or rehabilitate the body. Heat, electricity, motion, sound, water, and traction are among the most common therapies administered by trained professionals.

pacemaker: a natural or electrical regulator that controls the rhythm of an organ or bodily system; it is used most often to describe an artificial, electronically driven, device that keeps a defective heart pumping at a steady, "normal" rhythm, though pacemakers are also being adapted for other disease states.

phantom pain: the sensation that an amputated limb is still present and injured. Though the ends of nerves originally associated with the experience of pain may indeed be amputated, the brain may continue to receive messages from the remaining portions of the nerves. The result is real pain.

prosthesis, (pl. *prostheses*): an artificial substitute for a missing or diseased part of the body; the typical prosthesis is a portion of a leg and foot or an arm and hand.

stem cell: an embryonic all-purpose cell that is capable of growing into any of the body's 210 types of tissue. Stem cells have the potential to become repair kits, delivered by injection to damaged sites where they integrate with existing cells, obey local signals, and add to or replace diseased cells, as in the heart or kidney.

transplant: a tissue or organ that is transferred from one part of the body to another, or from one individual to another, and reconnected or grafted so as to function more or less normally.

UNOS: abbreviation for United Network for Organ Sharing, a national clearing house that maintains a computer listing of all persons in the United States deemed suitable candidates for organ transplants. UNOS matches candidates with compatible donations as they become available. Some 25 separate organs or tissues are matched in this manner.

xenograft or *xenotransplant*: a graft or transplant taken from one animal species and inserted into another species, particularly into a human when human donor parts are not available.

SELECTED BIBLIOGRAPHY

Adams, George Worthington, *Doctors in Blue: The Medical History of the Union Army in the Civil War*. New York: Henry Schuman, 1952.

Acierno, Louis J., *The History of Cardiology*. London: Parthenon Publishing Group, 1994.

Ackerman, Diane, *A Natural History of The Senses*. New York: Vintage Books, 1990.

American Medical Association, Charles B. Clayman, M.D., Medical Editor, *Home Medical Encyclopedia*. New York: Random House, 1989.

Barker, Wiley F. ,M.D. Clio: *The Arteries, The Development of Ideas in Arterial Surgery*. Austin, TX: R. G. Landes Co., 1992.

Brooks, Stewart, *Civil War Medicine*. Springfield, IL: Thomas Books, 1965.

Bruno, Leonard C., *The Landmarks of Science*, Washington, D.C.: Library of Congress/Facts On File, 1987.

Bunch, Bryan, *Handbook of Current Health & Medicine*, New York: Gale Research Inc., 1994.

Davis, Audrey B., *Triumph Over Disability: The Development of Rehabilitation Medicine in the U.S.A.* Washington, D.C.: Smithsonian Museum, Division of Medical Sciences, National Museum of History and Technology, Smithsonian Institution, 1973.

Devine, Edward, T. and The Carnegie Endowment for International Peace, *Disabled Soldiers and Sailors Pensions and Training*. New York: Oxford University Press, 1919.

Duffy, John, *The Healers, A History of American Medicine*. Urbana, IL: University of Chicago Press, 1976.

Flaste, Richard, *Medicine's Great Journey: One Hundred Years of Healing*. Boston: Little, Brown & Co., 1992.

Fye, W. Bruce, *American Cardiology: The History of a Specialty and Its College*. Baltimore: The Johns Hopkins University Press, 1996.

Garrison, Fielding H., *An Introduction to the History of Medicine*. Philadelphia: W.B. Saunders Co., 1929.

Hackett, Earle, *Blood: The Biology, Pathology, and Mythology*. New York: Saturday Review Press, 1973.

155

Haeger, Knut, *The Illustrated History of Surgery*. New York: Bell Publishing Co., 1988.

Lyons, Albert S., M.D. and R. J. Petrucelli II, M.D., *Medicine: An Illustrated History*, New York: Abradale Press & Harry N. Abrams, 1987.

McGrew, Roderick E., *Encyclopedia of Medical History*. New York: McGraw-Hill Book Co., 1985.

Murphy, Wendy B., *Healing the Generations*. Old Lyme, CT: American Physical Therapy Association and The Greenwich Publishing Group, Inc., 1995.

Murphy, Wendy B., *The Healing Heart*. Greenwich, CT: Clinical Communications, Inc., 1998.

Porter, Ray, *The Greatest Benefit to Mankind*. New York: W.W. Norton, 1997.

Rose, G. K., OBE, FRCS, *Orthotics Principles and Practice*. London: William Heinemann Medical Books, 1986.

Rutkow, Ira M. M.D., *Surgery: An Illustrated History*. St. Louis: Mosby-Year Book Inc., 1993.

Travers, B., ed., *World of Invention*. New York: Gale Research Inc., 1994.

Williams, Guy, *The Age of Agony: The Art of Healing 1700–1800*, Chicago: Academy Publishers, 1986.

Williams, Guy, *The Age of Miracles: Medicine and Surgery in the Nineteenth Century*, Chicago: Academy Publishers, 1987.

Wilson, A. B. Jr., "History of Amputation Surgery and Prosthetics," in J.H. Bowker and J.W. Michael, eds., *Atlas of Limb Prosthetics*, St. Louis: C. V. Mosby, 1989.

INDEX